THE ORCA METHOD ™

THE ORCA METHOD ™

9 simple steps to transform your english accent

Andrew Miziniak

Get more know-how at: OrcaMethod.com
ISBN-10: 0692607641 ISBN-13: 9780692607640 (Andrew Miziniak)
Library of Congress Control Number: 2016903386
Andrew Miziniak, Princeton, NJ

Cover Design by Mena Fusco
Individual Results may vary.

To Susan, Alexander & Katherine.

Introduction

Everyone in Princeton, New Jersey can speak Japanese.

I should clarify by saying 100% of the people I talked to on the streets of Princeton, NJ could speak Japanese.

Out of context, the immediate reaction to such a bold and seemingly outlandish statement is most likely disbelief, and in most cases, rightly so. But in this case, it just happens to be true. I went out on the streets of Princeton to conduct a test with a simple question - could I get people who did not know any Japanese to speak as if they were native speakers?

The experiment was an exercise to test a premise about accents and the way we teach people to speak English. I wanted to see if a person could repeat a phrase in Japanese that they had never heard before. I asked each person to repeat the words "*gochisosama deshita,*" a phrase that translates to "it was quite a feast" and is said after a meal. But what the words mean is irrelevant. I was only interested in how many people could speak those words and how quickly it took a person to produce the correct sounds.

I went about this by approaching people at random on the street. I eliminated those who had previous exposure to Japanese. At the end of the day, I had spoken to 100 people who knew nothing about the Japanese language, and I had run my test with each one.

I spoke the phrase "*gochisosama deshita*" and asked the person to repeat exactly what they had heard. Many people correctly repeated the words on the first try. Others got it on the second, and a few took a couple more tries to get the exact sounds. Eventually every single person got it right.

Everyone I tested was able to say "*gochisosama deshita.*" And what does this prove? Does each person in Princeton actually speak Japanese? No. But each person I tested could repeat the words and produce the sounds necessary to say a Japanese phrase they had never heard before and sound fluent doing so.

My main goal was to prove a larger and more critical point. I wanted to show that the way we teach people to speak English fluently is wrong. I wanted to show that the model for accent reduction currently used by millions of teachers around the world is not working for their students. Thousands of companies have made billions from the stated goal of helping people improve their accents, but many students are left having learned the language without the skills they need to truly feel as if they can speak fluently. There is no need for that to continue to be the case. I want to help people speak English fluently, faster, and easier than ever before.

This small test demonstrates everything I have questioned for years about the way we teach language and accent reduction. You see, I used to work for one of the largest training & development education company in the world, where I oversaw the delivery of hundreds of thousands of hours of language training during my career.

What worried me in all my years at the company was our *inability* to fix people's accents. It's true we "taught" people English, but when they came to us with accent problems, we had no clue about how to fix their accents, or what I call Fluidity.

Keep in mind that this was at one of most reputable language training companies in the world. Don't get me wrong, the company was the best at what it did. The teachers all cared very much about the students. The management, at least when I was there, was also consumed with a passion for teaching about language and cultures. The basis of all the lessons and techniques were built on what is called the "direct method." And this method is proven to work amazingly well to "teach" you a language.

When it came to accent reduction and fluidity, however, I was concerned we were not giving the students the tools they needed to speak the language fluently and were instead leaving them to fend for themselves with what the company had "taught" them about English.

I don't blame the company – students showed up at our doorstep with cash in hand, desperate to learn English and fix their accents. So what did we do? We gave them excellent teachers, a wonderful learning environment, took their money, and had absolutely no idea about how we were going to fix their accents. *We hadn't been taught how to do that.* The main techniques used to simply teach the English language remain unparalleled, despite their lack of attention to accent reduction.

I still, even to this day as a CEO of a language & cultural training company, fully acknowledge their effectiveness to teach the language. I used these methods in my own company on thousands of students, teaching them languages faster than with anything else. It just works.

But it doesn't work for accents.

The real question should be – what good is teaching someone the knowledge of a language if their lack of confidence about being able to speak fluently holds them back? It is akin to learning all there is to know about football, the strategies and techniques, but not actually being able to play.

I grew up in 4 countries and learned 5+ languages along the way. Unlike me, my parents didn't have the luxury of being taught the local language in school in each country; they learned it from books and along the way. And my parents had strong accents. I would sometimes joke that, even though they could both speak 6-8 languages, they spoke each language with the wrong accent – English with a Polish accent, French with an Italian accent, and German with a French accent.

Because I had been exposed to so many different languages, I assumed this was normal. I expected to hear a person speak with a different accent. I assumed it was how things were for people who learned English later in life or for those who did not have a chance to communicate with native speakers. I found this amusing until I matured enough to realize that their accent in each language was really getting in the way of their comfort and confidence in speaking to others.

Both my parents are well educated and well traveled. They can hold a conversation about any topic with anyone, so it was difficult to see them not be able to "fix" their level of communication quality. And certainly they tried when I was growing up – either by coming to me and asking how something was pronounced or by taking classes to help improve their skills. Nothing worked. And remember, they were fluent in each language. This was not a case where someone doesn't know the language and needs to be "taught." This was an issue with general fluidity where the person is conversational or better, but still carries the pronunciation patterns of their native tongue, or in my parent's case, a mix of several. It didn't make sense to me why there was such a struggle and why there was no way to fix the problem. I was on the path to develop the Orca Method, I just hadn't realized it yet.

And then, in my early teens when I was living in France, something happened that would change how I approached many of the new things in my life.

A friend invited me to meet a new kid. Let's call this new friend Ko. What struck me first was that Ko was an unbelievable guitarist. I was fascinated with music and had been stealing my brother's electric guitar to practice with every chance I could. My bother's guitar was a piece of junk. Imagine a fallen tree in the forest that someone has put strings on. That didn't bother me though; I brought it into Ko's room and started jamming with him.

And then Ko did something that blew me away. He played a beautiful and complex riff on the guitar at the same as he talked to my friend about where we were going that night. I couldn't believe it – he wasn't even looking down at what he was doing. He made what seemed to be incredibly difficult look effortless – so easy, so simple.

On that day I didn't say to myself that I wanted to play guitar the way he did – and 27 years later I still can't – what I decided was that from then on, I would do everything I did with the same grace and ease that I had just seen. I never again wanted to look at what I was doing; I wanted to experience it with my other senses. Literally, I wanted to be so good at things that I could talk about one thing while I was doing something else. I wanted to be able to spin those proverbial 12 plates while I ate lunch. I wanted to make everything I did look easy.

And then I understood the feeling that someone must have when they are trying to learn English. They want to be able to speak without having to think about how they sound or how others perceive them. They just want to have the confidence to use English the way they use their native tongue.

I wanted to find a solution. I didn't want to merely study and understand the problem; I wanted to find an easy solution. After years of playing guitar, piano, drums, bass, and recording 3 music albums on the side, along with years of speaking multiple languages, I felt I had developed a good ear for sound. I could hear patterns that others couldn't. I realized I could try a new approach.

Growing up, I did not just learn the vocabulary and grammar of each new language; I learned how to imitate their accents. For example, once I'd learned some German or Japanese or French, I could speak in English with a totally Japanese or French accent. But the words I said were English words. I got to thinking – if I can speak English and sound convincingly Japanese, why can't someone learn American English in a way that allows them to sound convincingly American? After all, the actual sound of the speech has nothing to do with grammar and vocabulary – it has to do with the patterns that naturally occur in whatever language I am emulating.

When I started my own training & development business dealing specifically with language instruction, accent reduction, cultural communication and talent development, I wanted to change the way the world communicates. With languages, my focus kept coming back to the simple notion that imitating accents had nothing to do with the spoken language itself.

The result is the Orca Method, which is rooted in the naturally occurring sound patterns in the English language. The key is learning the correct patterns. Once learned, anyone can obtain the proverbial keys to the castle with respect to speaking English fluently.

With the goal of developing the easiest route to better spoken English, I set out to discover what those patterns were in the language. My research revealed more than 40 repeated sounds that make up almost the entirety of sounds used to speak English. Within this array of sounds, some were very familiar to the non-native speaker, while others were much more subtle. For someone trying to learn English, knowing they would have to learn 40 new sounds would seem like a daunting task. They already have enough on their plate just learning the language. But what I found encouraging in the research was that of those 40 sounds, 9 patterns existed in approximately 70 percent of the most commonly spoken words in the English language. In the thousands of most often used words, 9 sound patterns repeated over and over. I concluded that by focusing on teaching just those 9 sound patterns, we could help people fix 70% of their spoken English, and 9 sounds would be much easier to learn than 40.

But that was only half the equation. That was just the data. The real question was how could we teach those sounds in the easiest and most comprehensive way to produce real world results?

The answer to our question takes us back to Princeton, NJ.

You see, when we asked people to repeat the Japanese word, we were looking for our answer. The answer is that all people, given some time, can imitate and reproduce sounds. On the surface, this may seem benign enough, but it is a mistake that millions of English language students make without realizing the consequences. And because of this error, the hard earned money they spend on English language classes produces very little, if any, results to improve their accent.

Here's what typically happens in an English class. The student – let's call him Victor – comes into class and has a strong eastern European accent. Victor has a "conversational" exchange with the teacher who is looking for pronunciation issues.

Victor says in a strong eastern accent – "Yesterday I went home and..."

At this point the teacher interrupts because Victor said the word "home" with a flat O. The teacher corrects Victor with a very round American "O" and says, "I went hOme."

Victor then does exactly what everyone in the Princeton test did – he repeats the word, pronouncing it the way the teacher did. He sounds great and he feels good. The class seems to be working. The teacher caught the mistake and seems to be doing a great job. The teacher jots down the progress and feels proud.

The next day Victor comes in and says, "Yesterday, I went home" with a flat O. The same as one day before. What happened? Both Victor and the teacher now feel disappointed and deflated. Victor thinks it's a memory problem and tries harder. And he still forgets.

This happens in millions of English classes around the world and it has probably happened to you. The simple fact is:

Vocal corrections don't work!

Just as the Princetonites repeated the word and forgot it the next day, when you vocally correct a student's pronunciation, the student *cannot* learn. If accent reduction programs worked, every single English student would no longer be going to classes. They would be done. I don't blame the students or teachers. The students want help and are willing to pay. The teachers sound convincing and are willing to get paid. As long as you treat the symptoms and not the disease, the symptoms keep coming back.

I had to find a solution to the problem that verbal accent corrections simply do not work. I wanted to put a space between the student and the teacher that allowed for corrections without the need to actually say the sound.

And one day, while playing some piano, it dawned on me. Eureka! I put my finger on the piano and said to myself "I can get to any note simply by telling myself to go up or down on these keys." I wouldn't have to say the sound or sing it. I could simply just say go up or go down and eventually find the sound. The Orchestration Correction Approach, or Orca Method, was becoming a reality.

By creating an interface between the student and the teacher, we could create a visual *keyboard* and correct the student by using "triggers," or simply predetermined gestures, symbols, and buzzwords, to make the correction. We already know that providing students just the sound doesn't work because they simply repeat it and then forget it the next day. The triggers give a teacher the ability to force the student to locate and make the sound on their own. The teacher is like a maestro telling the student what to do.

And, the ability to make the student create the sounds isn't limited to just one specific word or situation. There are so many sounds in the English language that come from words that are spelled differently. For example:

Susan

Tenet

Shin

Business

Information

Each of the underlined sounds above is identical: they sound like Y.

Perhaps it would be easier to her the sound if we replaced the letter s with Y: SusYn, TenYt, ShYn, BYsinYss, InformatYon

The Orca Method allows the instructor to help the student create the sounds themselves, regardless of where the sounds are present. If the teacher could use one gesture, a wave of the hand down for example, to represent the "Y" sound, they would be able to correct hundreds of words with the same gesture instead of having the student practice each word individually. That saves vast time and resources.

The power of the Orca Method is its focus on the major sound patterns coupled with triggers that allow the student to create the sounds on their own. Focusing on the patterns that occur most often, a student is able to cover the vast majority of words they will use in their everyday life. In addition, by creating the sounds themselves, they build their mental muscle memory to recreate the proper sounds when needed – at a much quicker pace.

Since I began applying the Orca Method in my work, we have been able to help our students in thousands of hours of English accent lessons. My hope is, as a reader of this book, you will also be able to apply the skills and techniques in your own life – either with your own teacher, one of ours, or even by yourself – to help bring you a more rewarding experience with the English language.

Chapter 1
The Orca Method™

Take a look at the text below. It demonstrates how powerful the Orca Method will be in helping you fix your English accent forever.

Each underlined portion of a word represents one of the sound patterns being identified. The word is also bolded to show you how many words are affected by the patterns in the ORCA Method. In the first text, where only one sound pattern is bolded, you can see how much of your English can be corrected by remembering *just one* correction for a single sound pattern. The second paragraph shows that same text with all 12 sound patterns underlined throughout.

ONE PATTERN

"When you can't **reduce** or **reuse**, **recycle**. **Any** household item that no longer has a place around your home might just **fit** the **bill** for some other household and **enjoy** a much longer useful life. The U.S. Environmental **Protection Agency** says that **recycling** saved over 72 **million** tons of trash from **landfills in 2003**, and **it creates millions** of jobs, **reduces greenhouse gases**, saves **energy** and natural **resources** and **decreases pollution**. **Items** that can't be **refurbished** are **remade into** new objects with high **percentages** of post-consumer **recycled material**. So **recycle** your castoffs, and **keep** the cycle **going** by **purchasing recycled** products". [1]

ADD 8 MORE AND VOILA!

"When you can't **reduce or reuse**, **recycle**. **Any household item that no longer has a place around your home** might **just fit the bill** for **some other household and enjoy a much longer useful** life. **The U.S. Environmental Protection Agency says that recycling saved over 72 million tons of trash from landfills in 2003, and it creates millions of jobs, reduces greenhouse gases, saves energy** and **natural resources** and **decreases pollution. Items that** can't **be refurbished are remade into new objects with** high **percentages of post-consumer recycled material. So recycle your castoffs**, and **keep the cycle going** by **purchasing recycled products"**.[1]

REFERENCE:

1. "List of Recyclable Household Items": SF Gate, accessed January, 17, 2015, http://homeguides.sfgate.com/list-recyclable-household-items-78711.html.

Remember, the underlined portion of the text represents the pattern and the bold represents the word it affects. If I were to tell someone they could fix the majority of their issues with their accent and pronunciation using just 9 patterns, they most likely wouldn't believe me. But it's true. Instead of memorizing thousands of words and dealing with thousands of corrections – not to mention the time and money you'll spend – you can just focus on 9 patterns.

As you can see from the second text, however, applying all 9 patterns illustrates that these sounds in some way have an effect on almost every single word. Think about the impact that applying the ORCA Method can have as these sounds appear in so much of the English language. Applying these techniques will help you speak in a more consistent and correct manner.

The process for learning how to produce these sounds on your own has been divided into three steps and each of these will be repeated for each sound.

The 3 Steps of ORCA Method

STEP 1 - IDENTIFICATION

Identification is the process of teaching the specific sound for the first time. This most resembles what happens in a typical English class where the teacher creates the sound and asks you to repeat it. This initial step is important to *teach* a sound so you know the exact sound you are trying to produce. Traditionally, teachers stop at Step 1. But Identification alone is useless for ongoing corrections of pronunciation problems. Just *giving* the student the sound doesn't fix their accent, but it is necessary to get the process started.

However, before moving on to the next step, it is important that you have mastered the identification of the specific sound. It is crucial to be able to identify the correct sound because starting with the wrong sound will only reinforce the incorrect accent and slow down or stall the learning process. Our rule is that you stay at Identification until you are absolutely certain you can create the sound before you move on to the next step.

STEP 2 - ASSOCIATION

Association takes the sound learned in the Identification phase (Step 1) and associates that sound with a specific trigger; a hand gesture, symbol, or buzzword. For the Y sound, I may tell the student that I will use the buzzword "go lower" while I wave my hand in a downward motion. We can also use a trigger:

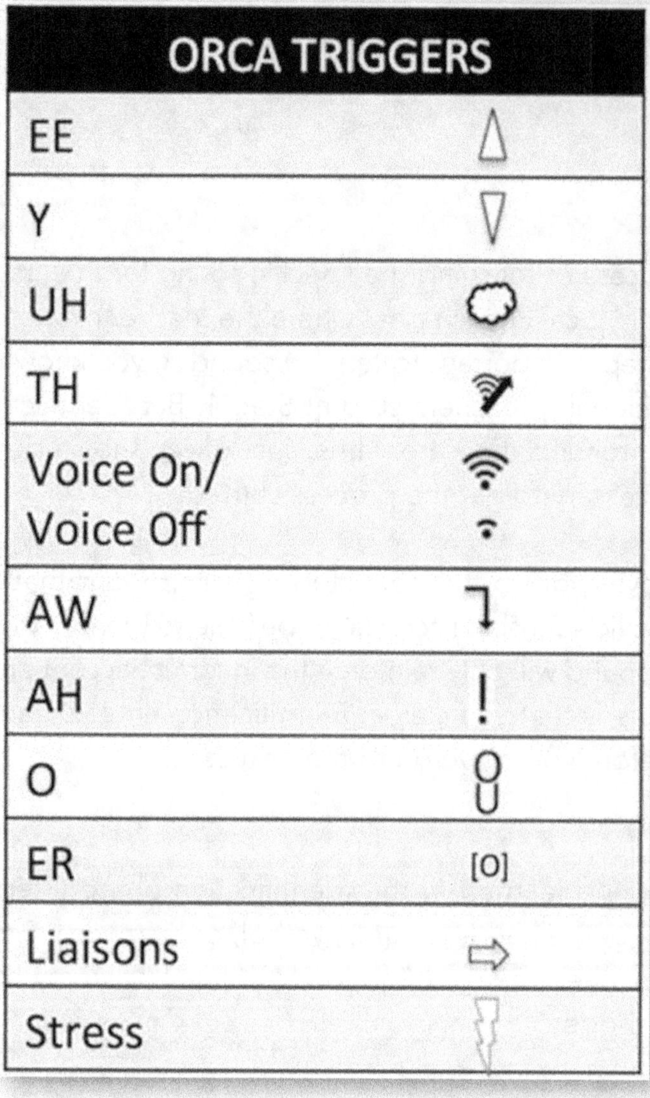

ORCA TRIGGERS	
EE	Δ
Y	∇
UH	
TH	
Voice On/ Voice Off	
AW	
AH	!
O	
ER	[O]
Liaisons	⇨
Stress	

The associated trigger incorporates variations of intensity in order to guide the student. With the example of the Y sound, the teacher is able to continue to tell the student to go lower or higher and guide them with the associated hand gesture if they are not producing the correct sound. They can gesture or say "even higher" or "much lower" to gain the added intensity and to focus in exactly on the sound just as you would go up and down the keys on a piano. With text, the trigger will indicate the general direction of the sound but can not have the variations that a teacher could use to assist in triggering the correct sound.

Once the student understands and remembers the connection between the sound pattern and the associated symbol, gesture, or buzzword, the teacher stops providing the sound and only uses the trigger or buzzword to get the student to produce the correct sound. This is why it is crucial for the student to have mastered the identification of the sound in Step 1 before progressing to Step 2.

STEP 3 - APPLICATION

This step is where the fun really begins and what makes the Orca Method unique. No one else teaches accents like this!

You can apply the method on your own or get help with a certified ORCA teacher to correct you. A teacher can have a student read any text or just speak out loud about any subject. As the student speaks, instead of jumping in when a mistake is made, the teacher uses the trigger, either a hand gesture, a buzzword, or symbol to prompt and help the student correct their own mistake in real time. Not only does the student self-correct, they do so without being given the correct sound they are trying to create – they receive only orchestrated triggers and buzzwords. In our online program at OrcaMethod.com, and in this book, we use trigger symbols, but the student can use hand gestures or buzzwords with your teacher. It doesn't actually matter what the trigger is as long as there is a trigger and that it stays consistent throughout your learning. This is important as some students may feel more comfortable in creating their own reference letters based on their own language and experience and not just have to use ours.

In this book you will learn techniques about sound *Identification* and *Association*. The final *Application* phase can be done by yourself, with your teacher, or with one of our certified trainers at OrcaMethod.com

With ORCA at the Application Phase, you can speak at a causal pace about anything you wish while your teacher corrects the relevant sounds at the relevant times. Keep in mind that the same sound exists in many words that are not always apparent, so the use of a trigger and orchestration is *essential* for you to learn to speak with confidence.

A student may say "Pol**a**nd" (emphasizing the letter a) and the teacher says, "End of word go lower" while waving their hand down to indicate it is actually a Y sound. The student corrects the word to sound like "Pol**y**nd." It doesn't look that way spelled out on paper, but Poland ends with the same sound as the word IN (not the word AND).

My mother, who always pronounced Poland as "Po*LAND*" with an eastern accent, always had trouble with the Y sound.

I taught her to first identify the Y sound correctly. Then I associated the sound and told her that whenever she saw the associated gesture or trigger, the sound would be Y. Then when I asked her where she was born she said "Pol**A**nd."

I immediately waved my hand down and said, "End of the word, go lower" and she, after a lifetime of mispronouncing the name of the country where she was born, impeccably and perfectly self-corrected and said the word Poland in a perfect American accent. She said PolYnd. She didn't sound like my mother! I was so used to her accent and its pattern, it was incredible.

If you are tired of trying to fix your accent but feel as if you aren't making progress and are finally ready to make a change, use the methods in this book to begin the process of finally improving your English.

Don't worry if you feel your accent cannot be fixed. I've worked with people at every level of English imaginable and have always seen improvement.

Don't go to another English class to learn about your accent. Imagine a child on a bicycle. He knows nothing of physics, mathematics, circumference, drag, or velocity – but he does know how to ride a bike.

Now imagine that you knew all of those things, the physics, the math, but you couldn't ride a bike! That's how millions of people feel when studying English around this world; they know everything there is to know about English, but don't feel confident enough to speak in a great English accent.

There should be an easier way. The Orca Method is the solution.

Now you can teach yourself on your own, with your own teacher, or with one of ours. Each of the following chapters is dedicated to one of the 9 sound patterns. Each chapter will go over the sound, illustrate examples of where the sound exists in different words, and provide texts for you to practice identifying and producing the sounds.

In order to help jumpstart your learning process, head to OrcaMethod.com. There you will find an online practice to help you with the identification phase for each sound, answer keys to the practice tests and – if you want immediate help – the ability to sign up for coaching sessions with one of our certified trainers.

NOTE TO STUDENT/READER:

As you work through this book, keep in mind it is meant as an active workbook for you to write it as it accompanies the content on the website. We recommend using a pencil so you can update your corrections as you progress through the sounds and patterns.

9 Sounds & Patterns

The following list includes the 9 sounds & patterns along with 2 subset exercises that assist in the Identification Phase of the main sound.

- **EE & Y**
  "He's been living here for fifteen years."
- **TH**
  "This is the theory that the Professor created with the help of that book."
  - **Voice On / Voice Off**
    "Susan's sister seemed so successful so we shared each other's ideas about the houses we were busy selling."
    "The first vow is very important at a formal event like a wedding"
- **AW**
  "I made all the calls to the mall because I needed to buy a small picture for my wall."
- **AH**
  "There's no obligation to stop hopping with your father."
- **UGH**
  "In my opinion, a thug can't understand when enough is enough."
- **O**
  "The only open window was broken with one stone or by a strongly blowing wind."
- **ER**
  "The man took the hat off his head, stepped over a happy-looking animal on the placemat, and entered the mansion."

  TR DR Rule

  - "Trevor's teacher trained a truck driver how to introduce a dry topic about dried out tree trunks and dripping drains."
- **LIAISONS**
- **STRESS**

ORCA TRIGGERS	
EE	△
Y	▽
UH	
TH	
Voice On/ Voice Off	
AW	
AH	!
O	
ER	[O]
Liaisons	⇨
Stress	

EE VS. Y

To illustrate the simplicity of the Orca Method, we will begin with the Y and the EE sounds (as heard in the words "this" and "need" respectively).

Speech pathologists will tell you that there are around 5 or 6 variations of just the EE sound in English. Sure, you can study phonetics from a phonetic dictionary, but what really matters is what the other speaker hears. The following is a variation list a phonetic instructor might have you memorize. Note that a non-ORCA teacher would try to have you memorize which words fall into which sounds.

- **/e_e/:**
  athlete, compete, complete, concrete, delete, eve, even, fever, grieve, here, meter, Pete, precede, scene, Steve, theme,
- **/ee/:**
  asleep, bee, beech, beef, beep, beer, beet, beetle, between, bleed, breed, breeze, bumblebee, career, cheek, cheer, cheese, cheetah, chimpanzee, creek, creep, coffee, deed, deep, deer, degree, discreet, eel, eerie, employee, engineer, exceed, fee, feeble, feed, feel, feet, flee, fleece, fleet, free, freeze, geese, glee, greed, green, greet, guarantee, heel, indeed, jeep, jeer, keel, keen, keep, knee, kneel, meek, meet, need, needle, peed, peek, peel, peep, peer, pioneer, preen, wheels, queen, reed, reef, reel, screech, screen, see, seed, seek, seem, seen, seep, seesaw, sheep, sheer, sheet, sleek, sleep, sleet, sleeve, sneeze, speech, speed, spree, squeeze, steel, steeple, steer, street, succeed, sweep, sweet, team, teen, teenager, teeth, three, tree, tweed, tweezers, reel, weed, week, weep, wheel, wheeze, zookeeper
- **/ea/:**
  beach, beacon, bead, beak, beam, beans, beard, beast, beat, beaver, beneath, between, bleach, bleak, bleat, breathe, cease, cheap, clean, clear, conceal, creak, cream, crease, creature, deal, dean, dear, decrease, defeat, dream, dreary, each, eager, eagle, ear, ease, east, Easter, eat, fear, feast, feat, feature, flea, freak, gear, gleam, glean, grease, heal, heap, hear, heat, heath, increase, jeans, knead, leach, lead, leader, leaf, league, leak, lean, leap, lease, leash, least, leaves, meal, mean, meat, meatball, measles, meat, near, neat, ordeal, pea, peace, peach, peal, peak, peanut, peat, plea, plead, please, pleat, preach, queasy, reach, read, real, really, reap, rear, reason, release, repeat, retreat, reveal, sea, seal, seam, season, seashore, seat, Seattle, seatbelt, scream, sheaf, shear, sheath, smear, sneak, speak, spear, squeal, steam, steal, steam, streak, stream, tea, teach, teak,

teal, team, treason, treat, veal, weak, wean, weary, weasel, weave, weak, wheat, wreath, year, yeast, zeal

- **/ie/:**
  belief, believe, brief, chief, diesel, grieve, niece, piece, pier, pierce, priest, relief, shield, shriek, siege, species, thief, field, yield
- **/_y/:**
  city, pony, baby, tiny, lily, shiny, sleepy, puppy

Now that you've seen so many possible variations of one sound, you will be pleased (or relieved) to know that all of the sounds in the list above fall under the EE category and that, *from now on, there will be only 2 sounds, the EE as in "beer" and the Y as in "miss."*

Even more important is that there will never be a sound mixed between the two of these. Words will either be pronounced with an EE or with a Y. There is no mix of the two. In the hundreds of words above, your teacher would simply use one trigger, on correction, for all those words.

ISSUE

The functional issue with the EE vs the Y sound is that the student usually sticks to a safety zone: a sound usually located somewhere between an EE and a Y. The truth is that in spoken English, there should actually be no sound between the two. It should either be absolute EE or absolute Y.

INCORRECT USE OF EE & Y SOUNDS

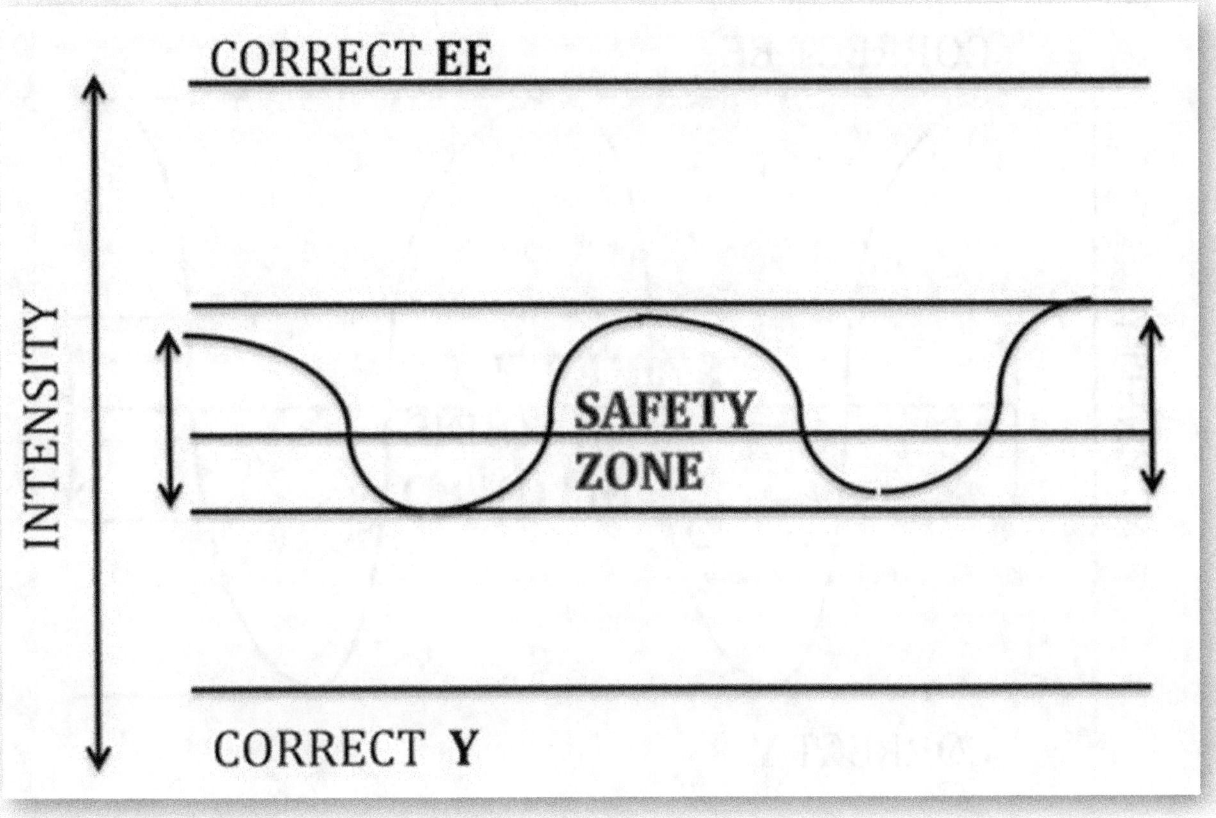

CORRECT USE OF EE & Y SOUNDS

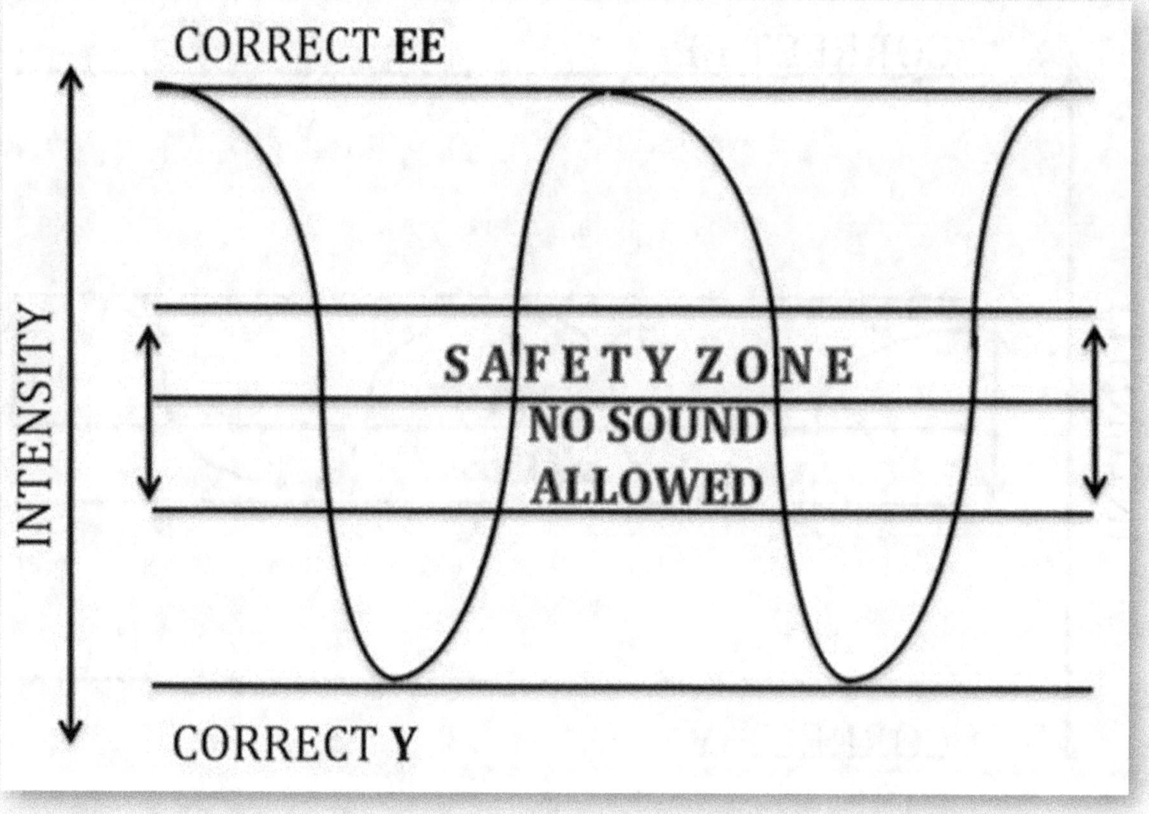

CAUTIONARY NOTE

Each Sound Pattern will have its own identification section. It is imperative that your teacher practice a specific technique with you during this phase. The technique consists of the teacher repeating your *incorrect* sound back to you and immediately afterward saying the correct sound. This should be automatically repeated at least three or four times so you can see the difference in the two sounds. You must also be comfortable with the teacher doing this and not feel offended because it will sound as if they are imitating you. You must be with a teacher you trust and one whose ear is good enough to repeat your incorrect sound. I would not trust an English teacher that could not repeat a student's incorrect sound because that would mean the teacher's ear sound reproduction ability was not good enough to fully assist with your accent reduction program.

Of course, having a teacher is not mandatory but since the identification phase is so important, we highly recommend it.

IDENTIFICATION

EE is identified first by trying to see if it exists in your root language. Many languages have the EE sound from "*chiba*" in Japanese, to "instituto" in Italian, to "*Kino*" in Polish. Keep in mind that you may want to lengthen the sound to twice as long as you would in your native tongue. Doing this will really differentiate it. So, instead of saying "cheese" try to say "cheeese."

If you already have the sound in your root language, your job is half complete. If you do not have the sound, you will need to locate it and practice with the repetitive corrections to establish a tonal relativity. This can be done with your own English tutor or online with one of our specialized virtual trainers.

EE is produced as a long sound. We exaggerate it to about 1 second long to emphasize its length. We also like to add a smile to the sound to express the height of the sound. The trigger for lengthening the EE is the teacher saying "Double Time." This will remind you to lengthen any sound you are producing.

Please refer to the sound in our practice section at OrcaMethod.com for assistance with sound identification.

Y is produced in the gut and is a singular sound. It must be as free of actual mouth sounds as possible. Most languages do not have the same exact Y as English, so your task will be to find it and practice it with your teacher before you can proceed to ORCA Phase 2.

EE & Y

ASSOCIATION

To the English teacher: EE is a double-time sound. We use 2 fingers to show double time, or we simply say "Double Time." We associate the sound to the buzz phrase "go higher" to contrast the Y "go lower" buzz phrase. The gesture of waving the hand upward to go higher can be used for EE and the gesture of waving the hand down used for Y. If you put 2 hands out, one about 12 inches above the other, you are indicating there is no sound in between. You can use the buzzword or phrase "be careful, there is no sound in between, go higher" for assistance. For our practice test, we will use the EE symbol but you will have to remember to make it longer (double time) yourself.

For Y, place your hand near your diaphragm to emphasize the guttural sound and keep explaining with words (not by correcting the sound with the correct sound) what should be done to achieve the correct sound.

ION RULE

For all words that end in ION, associate the correction with the term "ion rule." In our texts, we will simply put the trigger at the word but your teacher should remind you by saying "ION Rule" for you to make the correction.

This way, when the you make a mistake, your correction will not be waving your hand down to get the Y sound but rather a reminder that it is the "ION rule" to follow. This will let you try to find the sound on your own and reinforce the correction in a slightly different way.

Words like Constitution end with the Y sound.

Other examples (with the Y sound underlined):

administration
legislation
vacation
fortification

MENT RULE

For many words that end in MENT, associate the correction with the term "M-E-N-T rule." This way, when you make a mistake, the teacher's correction will not be waving their hand down to get the Y sound but rather a reminder that it is the "M-E-N-T rule" to follow. This will let you try to find the sound on your own using a slightly different trigger.

Words such as Government end with the Y sound. With that said, keep in mind that there will be some some words that are spelled with ENT at the end but do not actually produce the Y sound, such as in *Rent* or *Sent*. But your teacher will know which ones and will only trigger using the "M-E-N-T" rule or the Y trigger when applicable. That's the power of having an ORCA trainer to guide you.

Other examples (with the Y sound underlined):

solv<u>ent</u>
annulm<u>ent</u>
cog<u>ent</u>
segm<u>ent</u>
governm<u>ent</u>

FAST-SPEAK RULE

The Fast-Speak rule reminds the learner that the Y or EE sound may be more apparent in quick speech than in enunciated speech. An example of this is the word HARMONIZE.

Slowly spoken, there are no Y or EE sounds and the word sounds more like harm**O**nize.

In Fast-Speak however, the word is actually pronounced harm**Y**nize.

In cases where both sounds are possible depending on the pace of the conversation, we will choose the Fast-Speak version. In your practice tests, always assume fast-speak is what we are looking for. In some cases, we may skip a word if we feel the variation is too controversial and will leave it to your teacher to decide based on region and preference.

Let's take a look at a sample before we do a prep test.

Sentence:

He's been living here for fifteen years for business.

In this sentence, we typically hear students mixing up the EE and Y sounds to produce a more passive and indistinguishable sound that hovers toward the middle of the spectrum. We need the two sounds to be clearly different from each other. As you recall, there is no sound between the EE and the Y.

The **Bold** represents where the EE sound is heard and **Underlined Bold** where the Y sound is heard. For example:

H**E**'S B**EE**N L**I**V**I**NG H**E**RE FOR F**I**FT**EE**N Y**EA**RS FOR B**U**SIN**E**SS

The hand gesture, buzzword, or symbol pattern for only the EE and Y sounds should go as follows:

up, down, down, down, up, down, up, up, down, down.

Your teacher should correct you in this way and remind you that there are no sounds in between the two. All words will either be pronounced with a long EE or a Y.

INTRODUCING SYMBOLS

In the following examples, you'll see a triangle pointing up above the sound for EE and an triangle pointing down for the sound of Y. We have the audio available at OrcaMethod.com in the Practice area for you to compare. Try to pronounce the words while following the orchestration triggers to get the right feel. Pay special attention to words not spelled with the letter "I" but that have the Y sound.

Please note, there may be some words we choose to ignore either because they are pronounced differently in different regions or because they may play a role later on in our lessons. Use the Notes section to write down any questions you may have for your ORCA trainer later on.

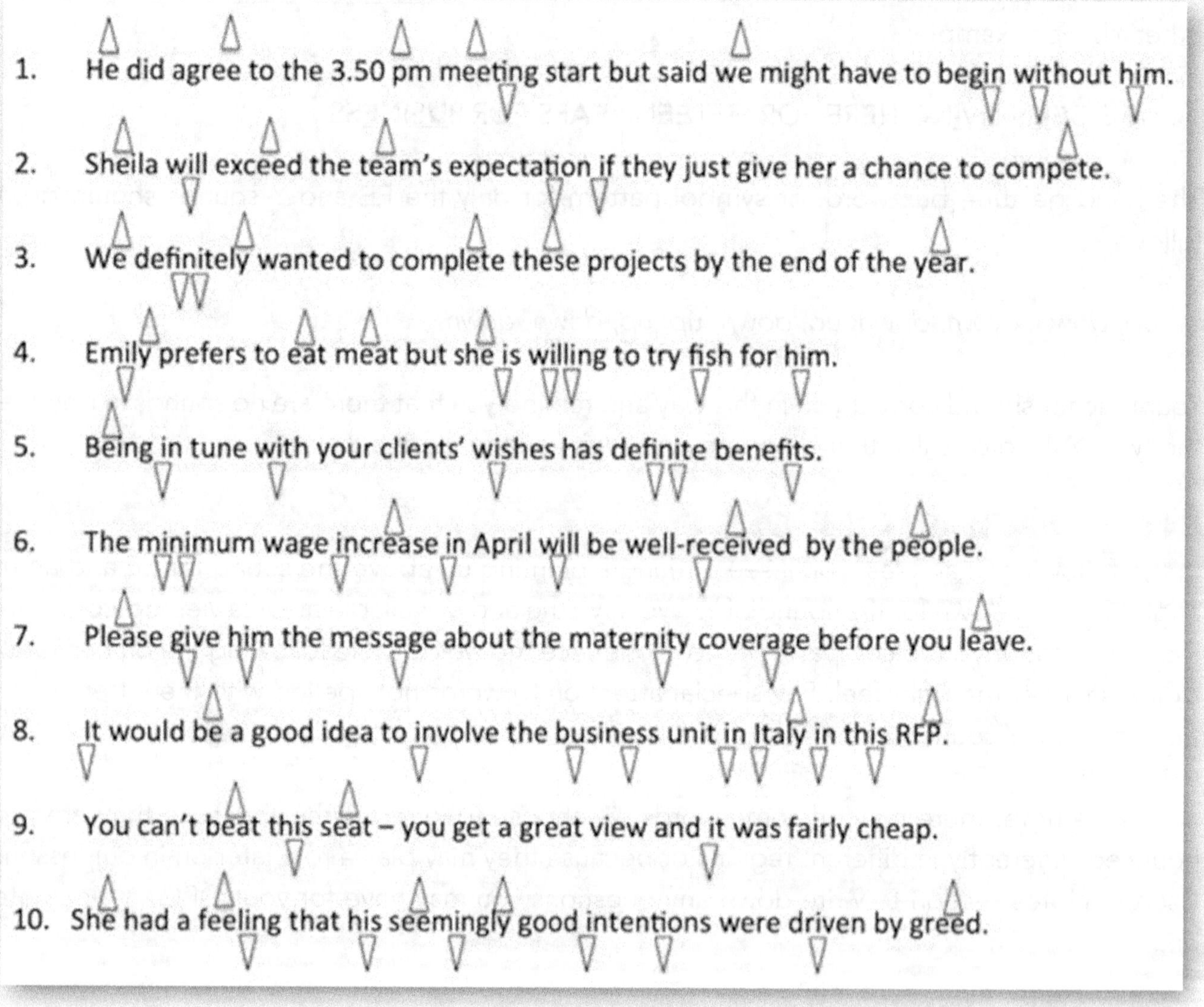

1. He did agree to the 3.50 pm meeting start but said we might have to begin without him.
2. Sheila will exceed the team's expectation if they just give her a chance to compete.
3. We definitely wanted to complete these projects by the end of the year.
4. Emily prefers to eat meat but she is willing to try fish for him.
5. Being in tune with your clients' wishes has definite benefits.
6. The minimum wage increase in April will be well-received by the people.
7. Please give him the message about the maternity coverage before you leave.
8. It would be a good idea to involve the business unit in Italy in this RFP.
9. You can't beat this seat – you get a great view and it was fairly cheap.
10. She had a feeling that his seemingly good intentions were driven by greed.

EE & Y ASSOCIATION QUIZ

Let's practice associating the pattern to the symbol. The answers appear on the following page.

Place an UP arrow above the EE sound and a DOWN arrow below for the Y sound. We have spaced the text so that you will have room to draw the symbol.

❖ ❖ ❖

So, what can you tell me about yourself?

Does this phrase sound familiar? Of course. It is the most frequently asked question in a new surrounding – if you are applying for a job or you have just started a new position but even when you meet your teacher for the first time, you can certainly expect this question.

Since people are going to form their opinion based on your answer, it is good to have an idea what you are going answer before the question is asked. Be prepared, write down what you are going to say, especially if you feel uncomfortable answering this question all the time, or you simply find it challenging to figure out what to say so that you give the right impression.

But how do you know what they want to hear? You don't. In fact, they probably don't have a clear idea what they would like to hear, either. They are simply interested in you and would like to get to know you better. Or, in the case of an interview or evaluation, for example, they pay attention not only to what you say but how you say it – what words, expressions you choose to use, how vague or detailed you are about different aspects of your life, whether or not you get into personal details or subjective matters. All this counts, and we have not even mentioned body language and tone of voice. A thorough interviewer forms his/her opinion by putting together these details. Most people, people who just would like to get to know you, do this subconsciously. They don't realize but they judge you based on all the above factors.

So, what can you tell me about yourself?

Does this phrase sound familiar? Of course. It is the most frequently asked questions in a new surrounding – if you are applying for a job or you have just started a new position but even when you meet your teacher for the first time, you can certainly expect this question.

Since people are going to form their opinion based on your answer, it is good to have an idea what you are going answer before the question is asked. Be prepared, write down what you are going to say, especially if you feel uncomfortable answering this question all the time, or you simply find it challenging to figure out what to say so that you give the right impression.

But how do you know what they want to hear? You don't. In fact, they probably don't have clear idea what they would like to hear, either. They are simply interested in you and would like to get to know you better. Or, in the case of an interview or evaluation, for example, they pay attention not only to what you say but how you say it – what words, expressions you choose to use, how vague or detailed you are about different aspects of your life, whether or not you get into personal details or subjective matters. All this counts, and we have not even mentioned body language and tone of voice. A thorough interviewer forms his/her opinion by putting together these details. Most people, people who just would like to get to know you, do this subconsciously. They don't realize but they judge you based on all the above factors.

In your accent reduction class, you will need to ask your teacher to find texts to read that include all the possible variations of Y that are not necessarily spelled with the letter "I." These may include the words person, tenet, organization, Susan, business, message, etc. Our ORCA trainers have all the available resources to help you with text specifically designed to get quick results.

CONTIGUOUS WORDS

* The "Contiguous Words" section will help you begin to consistently enunciate the sound without the context of the text. It is a force multiplier in that you can carry a similar, or easier to pronounce, version from one word to the next and assist you in consistently bringing a common tone to all the words. Please read the following words as if you are reading a full paragraph, without stopping, and try to make all the EE and Y sounds identical in each part. We have pulled the words that contain the sounds from the above exercise for you to practice, but it is a good idea to redo the quiz after practicing here to hear if you've improved. A word of caution: some of the words below may contain a mix of both EE and Y so you will have to choose which sound goes where.

EE (Read the following as if you are reading a sentence)

Me frequently even meet teacher certainly people be feel simply hear probably clear idea hear simply detailed people subconsciously realize

Y (Read the following as if you are reading a sentence)

This familiar it is frequently questions in surrounding applying position even certainly this question since going opinion it is going if answering this question simply it challenging figure give impression in simply interested in interview attention it expressions into subjective interviewer his this

IMPORTANT INFORMATION ABOUT PREP TESTS

The Prep Test has a longer text than you would usually find in an English training book. The reason for this is that we want the corrections to be remembered within the context of a story and not from some random sentences.

Stories invoke imagery, auditory cues, as well as kinesthetic responses, and only by delving into a bigger narrative does the mind create memories of what it has experienced. This way, by using a narrative to correct your English, you have a better chance of remembering the corrections. This longer text approach is a variation of a mnemonic device that has its roots in the "method of LOCI." Web search it – it's very interesting.

After each paragraph, there will be a *count* indicator as to how many of the sounds exist in that paragraph. Make sure you find all of them. Some words, such as the word *because* can be pronounced *bEEcause* or *bYcause*, depending on the person. With such a word, it is essential to place the symbol above and below to indicate the variability of the sound or we may simply leave it blank depending on the context.

We expect you to find at least 80% of the sounds in order to move on to the next sound or pattern in the system. The answers to the Prep tests are found on OrcaMethod.Com (in the practice section) and you can compare what you did in this workbook with the answer slide on the website. Our advice is to use a pencil so as to be able to do corrections as you improve.

EE & Y Prep Test

Instructions: Arrow DOWN for all the Y sounds and arrow UP for all the EE sounds in the following text. The number before each paragraph represents the slide number in the Practice Center at OrcaMethod.com. A sound count will appear at the bottom of each test to give you a hint on how many words possess the sound.

Excerpt from *The Unicultural Advantage* by Andrew Miziniak (EE & Y Slide 1-11)

EE & Y SLIDE 1

Culture shock can be experienced in any new environment, whether a person is at home, traveling to new destinations abroad, or in a new relationship. The way culture shock manifests will differ, however, depending on the person. I use two groups to identify how people deal with culture shock in new environments: Low and High Frequency individuals.

People fall into two groups based on how they experience and react to culture shock. What separates the two groups is how they manage expectations and deal with their satisfaction through what I call a Personal Inventory of Happiness. Consider what it means for you to be happy in your life. How a person manages their happiness is what makes them Low or High Frequency.

EE Count: 14
Y Count:40

EE & Y SLIDE 2

Low Frequency individuals are people who, over time, have dug very deeply into their personal inventory of happiness. They have accumulated many little things they feel make their life whole. The totality of those items brings them joy. From the way they set up their room in the morning to catch the first rays of sun, to their favorite brand of coffee, the garden they tend, their favorite barista at the coffee shop, and their favorite route to work to avoid traffic. Every little thing adds a bit of happiness.

EE Count: 12
Y Count: 24

EE & Y SLIDE 3

On the other side of the spectrum there are High Frequency Individuals. These people focus on a few simple items that bring them pleasure. Perhaps a laptop and Internet connection, their favorite book, or personal item is all that is required. But at the end of the day, as long as they have a roof over their heads and food on the table, these people will be all right anywhere.

EE Count: 7
Y Count: 15

EE & Y SLIDE 4

They don't seem affected coming and going out of their home environment because they seem to take their home with them wherever they go. While this person only has a few items they need to feel happy, they check on those items very often to make sure they are still present. Traveling or working in new environments abroad best illustrates the culture shock people normally experience because of the stark visible differences between cultures. New architecture, cuisine, entertainment, and language can create the feeling of being out of place.

EE Count: 16
Y Count: 29

EE & Y SLIDE 5

Low Frequency individuals are those who show more immediate symptoms of culture shock in new environments. When they arrive at their destination, everything is missing. The cramped hotel is nothing like their home, they are drinking coffee that tastes different, and their favorite people and places are gone. All of their senses are affected.

EE Count: 6
Y Count: 24

EE & Y SLIDE 6

When you spend a lifetime appreciating certain things, then find that those things are missing, you encounter a sinking feeling and home-sickness that can last for a couple of weeks, months, or for some people, years. The key here is the word **appreciating**. To appreciate is to grow in value. Low Frequency individuals have allowed the deep seeded elements of their happiness to grow in value over time. They may not have started out particularly passionate about any single element such as coffee or gardening, but those elements became much more important over time.

EE Count: 21
Y Count: 33

EE & Y SLIDE 7

Because culture shock for Low Frequency individuals manifests itself right away, it is cause for immediate concern. When a company relocates an employee overseas who experiences immediate culture shock, the company begins to worry that either the relocation was the wrong decision or they've picked the wrong person for the opportunity.

EE Count: 14
Y Count: 23

EE & Y SLIDE 8

While a Low Frequency person encounters culture shock soon upon arrival, their personal style of appreciating things over time can help them fill the gap the longer they stay, and as new elements take the place of the old. In a matter of a few weeks to a couple of months, the Low Frequency individual can learn to adapt and new items in their life will take the place of the elements they have missed. By spending time, sharing experiences, and interacting with the culture, they find new elements of happiness in a previously foreign world. The immediate culture shock will dissipate if the person can adapt to the new environment. This is where cultural support comes into play.

EE Count: 15
Y Count: 40

EE & Y SLIDE 9

High Frequency individuals exhibit little visible culture shock when entering new environments. These people only require a few key items to stay happy. As long as their basic needs are met, things seem to go according to plan. Because they do not exhibit immediate signs of culture shock, many companies tend to favor High Frequency individuals for international travel and relocation.

A High Frequency individual relocated to another country for work is fine upon arrival at the new destination. When HR asks if everything is okay, they respond that there are no issues. Relocation services may ask if they need a cultural program to help with the adjustment to a new environment, but the response will be they don't need it because everything is fine.

EE Count: 25
Y Count: 47

EE & T SLIDE 10

What many companies fail to realize is the potential long-term problems High Frequency individuals may face. As there were no immediate issues, the company assumes things will go according to plan. After a few months, everyone stops asking how things are going in the adjustment process. HR and Relocation services have already forgotten about the transition. But after having visited all the tourist attractions and satisfied the survival need for a roof over their heads and food on the table, what remains for the High Frequency individual? By not having invested in the very small appreciating aspects of a culture, new feelings of homesickness and emptiness may begin to creep up months or years after relocation. This delayed reaction to changes in the environment is what I call Latent Culture Shock. It can pose serious problems for corporate goals and objectives abroad.

EE Count: 24
Y Count: 52

EE & Y SLIDE 11

Imagine yourself as a High Frequency individual who is dealing with latent culture shock. When you were at home, the people around you may have provided you with the Low Frequency elements needed to harmonize your perspective to theirs. You may not have had a garden but your mom did, you may not have cared about what type of coffee you drank, but your friends always insisted on going to a particular cafe. You were interconnected and got to harmonize without needing to invest in your particular environment. But now that environment and support are missing.

EE Count: 8
Y Count: 34

ORCA TRIGGERS	
EE	△
Y	▽
UH	
TH	
Voice On/ Voice Off	
AW	
AH	!
O	O U
ER	[O]
Liaisons	⇨
Stress	

UH

IDENTIFICATION

The UH pattern is pronounced in the same way as a hesitating "umm" sound people make in between words. Just get rid of the M and do the UH sound to achieve the right tone. The "uhhhh" sound can be heard at OrcaMethod.com or have your teacher assist you to get it right before you continue.

Words that include the UH pattern include: under, fun, ability, thunder, cut, love.

CONTIGUOUS WORDS (REMEMBER TO READ AS IF YOU WERE READING A SENTENCE)

Does of the a applying the opinion idea the uncomfortable the but idea the attention subjective opinion subconsciously judge above

UH ASSOCIATION QUIZ

So, what can you tell me about yourself?

Does this phrase sound familiar? Of course. It is the most frequently asked question in a new surrounding – if you are applying for a job or you have just started a new position but even when you meet your teacher for the first time, you can certainly expect this question.

Since people are going to form their opinion based on your answer, it is good to have an idea what you are going answer before the question is asked. Be prepared, write down what you are going to say, especially if you feel uncomfortable answering this question all the time, or you simply find it challenging to figure out what to say so that you give the right impression.

But how do you know what they want to hear? You don't. In fact, they probably don't have a clear idea what they would like to hear, either. They are simply interested in you and would like to get to know you better. Or, in the case of an interview or evaluation, for example, they pay attention not only to what you say but how you say it – what words, expressions you choose to use, how vague or detailed you are about different aspects of your life, whether or not you get into personal details or subjective matters. All this counts, and we have not even mentioned body language and tone of voice. A thorough interviewer forms his/her opinion by putting together these details. Most people, people who just would like to get to know you, do this subconsciously. They don't realize but they judge you based on all the above factors.

So, what can you tell me about yourself?

Does this phrase sound familiar? Of course. It is the most frequently asked questions in a new surrounding – if you are applying for a job or you have just started a new position but even when you meet your teacher for the first time, you can certainly expect this question.

Since people are going to form their opinion based on your answer, it is good to have an idea what you are going answer before the question is asked. Be prepared, write down what you are going to say, especially if you feel uncomfortable answering this question all the time, or you simply find it challenging to figure out what to say so that you give the right impression.

But how do you know what they want to hear? You don't. In fact, they probably don't have clear idea what they would like to hear, either. They are simply interested in you and would like to get to know you better. Or, in the case of an interview or evaluation, for example, they pay attention not only to what you say but how you say it – what words, expressions you choose to use, how vague or detailed you are about different aspects of your life, whether or not you get into personal details or subjective matters. All this counts, and we have not even mentioned body language and tone of voice. A thorough interviewer forms his/her opinion by putting together these details. Most people, people who just would like to get to know you, do this subconsciously. They don't realize but they judge you based on all the above factors.

Excerpt from *The Unicultural Advantage* by Andrew Miziniak (UH Slide 1-5)

UH SLIDE 1

Transitory cultures instruct you to clearly identify yourself as an individual or a part of a small chosen collective. People in Transitory cultures pride themselves on their individuality. They will have more independent opinions and ideas. This will work better in think tanks and small teams. Studies have shown that individuals in Transitory cultures tend to be more innovative. This often happens in highly urban and diverse areas.

UH Count : 6

UH SLIDE 2

But over time this individuality is broken down by our willingness to be pack animals. Even those who take on the most radical and chic approach to life will eventually be followed by others who assimilate to them. Once an outlier, that person becomes the median.

Think about it: today, because everyone and everyone's mother has joined Facebook, the consensus among people is that there is something strange about you if you don't have an account. It is suspicious. The force of the collective is bearing down on you and telling you how to feel, which will change how you think, and subsequently even change what you see.

UH Count : 22

UH SLIDE 3

Complex cultures identify with the larger collective or groups. They are always aware of how their actions may impact their spouse, their company, their neighbors, their kids, their village and their country's reputation. If their mom told them it takes seven years to digest gum, the transfer of trust from the collective is so strong that they simply believe it. And believe it they will -- forever. That is an important distinction between collectives. One is a chosen collective while the other is imposed. For too long, cultural experts had been labeling China as a collective culture while completely ignoring the tens of thousands of chosen collectives in the United States.

UH Count : 20

UH SLIDE 4

Both Transitory and Complex cultures are essential to the survival of our species. When resources are low, the power of habit is what we need in order to notice changes and variations. By staying Transitory and trying to understand things we've already figured out, we not only waste energy, we miss potential new resources. What harm does it do if we believe George Washington had wooden teeth when it's not true? If it doesn't affect our resources, why should we pry open new understandings? It seems wasteful to the Complex cultures.

It is this dilemma that we face when things we once understood are relegated to the brain stem and become beliefs. Many of these beliefs seem quite benign at first. But as the global world interacts, many of our benign beliefs will need to be revisited and reevaluated because they may negatively impact interaction with another culture.

UH Count : 15

UH SLIDE 5

Think about the issue of human rights, rights of women and children around the world. Think about issues such as the glass ceiling, animal rights, gun laws, and the metric versus imperial system. The list could go on for miles. All these items desperately want to be defined, resolved, and go to sleep in the subconscious brain stem but need to be activated back into the Transitory cortex on a continual basis. Every once in a while, we must reevaluate our major belief systems. The trigger for this is usually a resource. This is why managing resources for a population is a key factor in maintaining order and balance in society. When resources become low, the unfortunate reaction of a culture is to use the "get back in your place" approach. Cultural interactions often resemble musical chairs. When resources are abundant we dance around, all the while keeping our eye on that chair in case the music stops. That's where our stereotypes come from; our need to keep order during the shuffle.

UH Count : 28

ORCA TRIGGERS	
EE	△
Y	▽
UH	
TH	
Voice On/ Voice Off	
AW	
AH	!
O	
ER	[O]
Liaisons	⇨
Stress	

Note: You may Skip Voice On Voice Off if you feel comfortable in producing these Voiced and Unvoiced sounds. It is included as a sub-lesson for helping you with the TH sound later on in our program. When you do the practice section of Voice On Voice Off, keep in mind it is meant to help you train your voice box to activate and is not one of our main sound patterns so you do not need to memorize the words associated as much as you would with the main sound patterns.

VOICE ON - VOICE OFF IDENTIFICATION

For the following sounds, a technique called VOICE ON VOICE OFF must be employed. Simply put, you make one of the two variations of the sound and then, with the same breath, turn your voice box on, then off, until you feel as if you are out of breath. (Take breaks and breathe often). Often, the solution to sounding clear in English is to radicalize the sound to either strong vocal or no vocal at all. ESL students will tend to mix and match.

So, in one breath you will say the S sound and, without restarting the breath, turn on your voice box to produce a Z sound. The same will be done with the letters F and V.

VOICE ON – VOICE OFF ASSOCIATION

Your teacher should remind you with the trigger "NOW VOICE OFF, NOW VOICE ON FOR THAT WORD," for example. As for symbols in the practice, we use a sound pulse (like a Wi-Fi signal) for Voice On and a small sound pulse for Voice off. Please reference the symbol key for more information.

The following sentences focus on a few of the Voice On Voice Off sounds we will be covering. They include:

S & Z
F & V

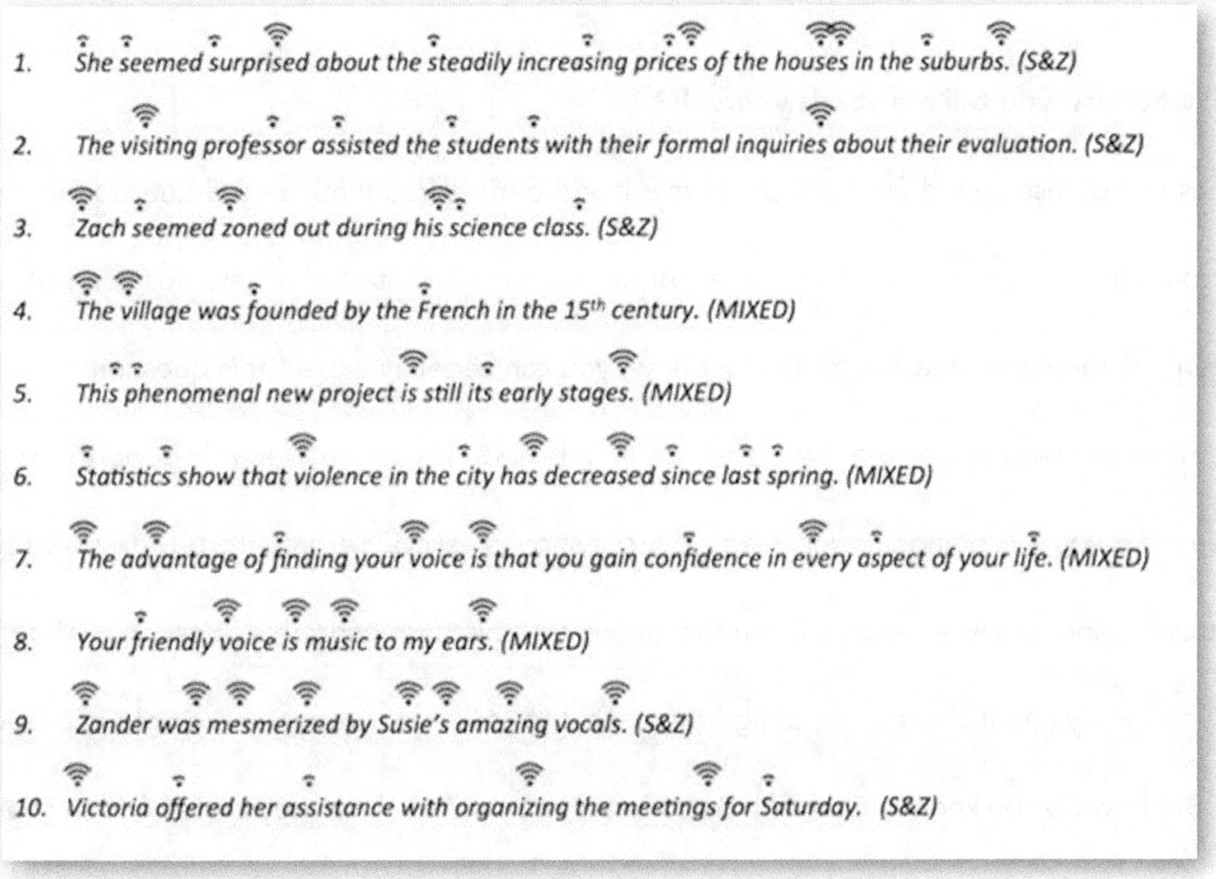

1. She seemed surprised about the steadily increasing prices of the houses in the suburbs. (S&Z)
2. The visiting professor assisted the students with their formal inquiries about their evaluation. (S&Z)
3. Zach seemed zoned out during his science class. (S&Z)
4. The village was founded by the French in the 15th century. (MIXED)
5. This phenomenal new project is still its early stages. (MIXED)
6. Statistics show that violence in the city has decreased since last spring. (MIXED)
7. The advantage of finding your voice is that you gain confidence in every aspect of your life. (MIXED)
8. Your friendly voice is music to my ears. (MIXED)
9. Zander was mesmerized by Susie's amazing vocals. (S&Z)
10. Victoria offered her assistance with organizing the meetings for Saturday. (S&Z)

CONTIGUOUS WORDS (REMEMBER TO READ AS IF YOU ARE READING A SENTENCE)

Voice Off

She seemed surprised steadily increasing prices suburbs professor assisted students seemed science class founded French this phenomenal still its statistics city since last spring finding aspect life friendly offered assistance Saturday

Voice On

Surprised prices houses suburbs visiting inquiries Zach zoned his village is stages violence has advantage voice is music ears is Zander was mesmerized Suzie's amazing vocals Victoria organizing meetings

NOTE: The TH sound will be avoided for now as it has its own section and exercises.

VOICE ON – VOICE OFF ASSOCIATION QUIZ

So, what can you tell me about yourself?

Does this phrase sound familiar? Of course. It is the most frequently asked question in a new surrounding – if you are applying for a job or you have just started a new position but even when you meet your teacher for the first time, you can certainly expect this question.

Since people are going to form their opinion based on your answer, it is good to have an idea what you are going answer before the question is asked. Be prepared, write down what you are going to say, especially if you feel uncomfortable answering this question all the time, or you simply find it challenging to figure out what to say so that you give the right impression.

But how do you know what they want to hear? You don't. In fact, they probably don't have a clear idea what they would like to hear, either. They are simply interested in you and would like to get to know you better. Or, in the case of an interview or evaluation, for example, they pay attention not only to what you say but how you say it – what words, expressions you choose to use, how vague or detailed you are about different aspects of your life, whether or not you get into personal details or subjective matters. All this counts, and we have not even mentioned body language and tone of voice. A thorough interviewer forms his/her opinion by putting together these details. Most people, people who just would like to get to know you, do this subconsciously. They don't realize but they judge you based on all the above factors.

So, what can you tell me about yourself?

Does this phrase sound familiar? Of course. It is the most frequently asked questions in a new surrounding – if you are applying for a job or you have just started a new position but even when you meet your teacher for the first time, you can certainly expect this question.

Since people are going to form their opinion based on your answer, it is good to have an idea what you are going answer before the question is asked. Be prepared, write down what you are going to say, especially if you feel uncomfortable answering this question all the time, or you simply find it challenging to figure out what to say so that you give the right impression.

But how do you know what they want to hear? You don't. In fact, they probably don't have clear idea what they would like to hear, either. They are simply interested in you and would like to get to know you better. Or, in the case of an interview or evaluation, for example, they pay attention not only to what you say but how you say it – what words, expressions you choose to use, how vague or detailed you are about different aspects of your life, whether or not you get into personal details or subjective matters. All this counts, and we have not even mentioned body language and tone of voice. A thorough interviewer forms his/her opinion by putting together these details. Most people, people who just would like to get to know you, do this subconsciously. They don't realize but they judge you based on all the above factors.

CONTIGUOUS WORDS (REMEMBER TO READ AS IF YOU ARE READING A SENTENCE)

Voice Off

So yourself sound familiar course most frequently asked surrounding if for just started for first this question since form based answer question asked say especially if feel uncomfortable answering this question simply find figure say so impression fact simply say different aspect life subjective this counts most just this subconsciously based

Voice On

Phrase is questions position even is have is give have interview evaluation words expressions choose use vague details subjective matters voice interviewer forms his these details above

VOICE ON VOICE OFF PREP TEST

Excerpt from *The Unicultural Advantage* by Andrew Miziniak (V on - V Off Slide 1-6)

Voice On Voice Off Slide 1

Just as *understandings* become *beliefs* over time, *individuals* become *groups*, and those groups tell us how we should feel. Complex cultures tend to be more collective. They will reward members of the culture for being a part of it and, in turn, allow for clear distinctions with people that are from outside of the culture. Think of Japan, where you are either Japanese or labeled a Gaijin or Gaikokujin, which translates to foreigner. There is a clear-cut distinction in Complex cultures between "us" and "them."

S COUNT: 11
Z COUNT: 11

NOW DO THE SAME FOR F & V

Voice On Voice Off Slide 2

Just as *understandings* become *beliefs* over time, *individuals* become *groups*, and those groups tell us how we should feel. Complex cultures tend to be more collective. They will reward members of the culture for being a part of it and, in turn, allow for clear distinctions with people that are from outside of the culture. Think of Japan, where you are either Japanese or labeled a Gaijin or Gaikokujin, which translates to foreigner. There is a clear-cut distinction in Complex cultures between "us" and "them."

S Count: 11
Z Count: 11
F Count: 3
V Count: 6

Voice On Voice Off Slide 3

Transitory cultures instruct you to clearly identify yourself as an individual or a part of a small chosen collective. People in Transitory cultures pride themselves on their individuality. They will have more independent opinions and ideas. This will work better in think tanks and small teams. Studies have shown that individuals in Transitory cultures tend to be more innovative. This often happens in highly urban and diverse areas. But over time this individuality is broken down by our willingness to be pack animals. Even those who take on the most radical and chic approach to life will eventually be followed by others who assimilate to them. Once an outlier, that person becomes the median.

S Count: 14
Z Count: 21
F Count: 4
V Count: 11

Voice On Voice Off Slide 4

Think about it: today, because everyone and everyone's mother has joined Facebook, the consensus among people is that there is something strange about you if you don't have an account. It is suspicious. The force of the collective is bearing down on you and telling you how to feel, which will change how you think, and subsequently even change what you see. Although we know that people in Columbus's day did not truly believe the earth was flat, we still cling to the stories we heard as children. While you know the commonly held belief is wrong, will you be the one to dispute it at every opportunity?

S Count: 13
Z Count: 12
F Count : 6
V Count: 8

NOTE: Now let's take what we know about S & Z and F & V and add the EE & Y symbols to the text in the following paragraph.

Voice On Voice Off Slide 5

Complex cultures identify themselves as a small part of the whole, as a collective. Transitory individuals may also be part of a collective, but it is usually one of a number of chosen collectives. Complex cultures don't mind forcing their collective beliefs on others to establish predictability.

That is an important distinction between collectives. One is a chosen collective while the other is imposed. For too long, cultural experts had been labeling China as a collective culture while completely ignoring the tens of thousands of chosen collectives in the United States.

S Count: 8
Z Count: 22
F Count: 3
V Count: 15
EE Count: 7
Y Count: 37

Voice On Voice Off Slide 6

Both Transitory and Complex cultures are essential to the survival of our species. When resources are low, the power of habit is what we need in order to notice changes and variations. By staying Transitory and trying to understand things we've already figured out, we not only waste energy, we miss potential new resources. What harm does it do if we believe George Washington had wooden teeth when it's not true? If it doesn't affect our resources, why should we pry open new understandings? It seems wasteful to the Complex cultures.

S Count: 12
Z Count: 15
F Count: 4
V Count: 6
EE Count: 17
Y Count: 25

ORCA TRIGGERS	
EE	△
Y	▽
UH	
TH	
Voice On/ Voice Off	
AW	
AH	!
O	O U
ER	[O]
Liaisons	⇨
Stress	

ISSUE

The student usually hears the final pop or burst of the TH sound, which to them is closest to a T or D in their language, depending on Voice On or Voice Off. Basically, "thanks" sounds like "tanks."

TH IDENTIFICATION

The key is to create a ½ second long TH sound that goes from barely imperceptible to a full finish. The wind up must be practiced over and over to reduce the D sound. Use every tactic possible to get the tongue in the right position between the teeth to produce a consistent yet increasing rate sound. If you need assistance, our ORCA Method Trainers are standing by at www. OrcaMethod.com.

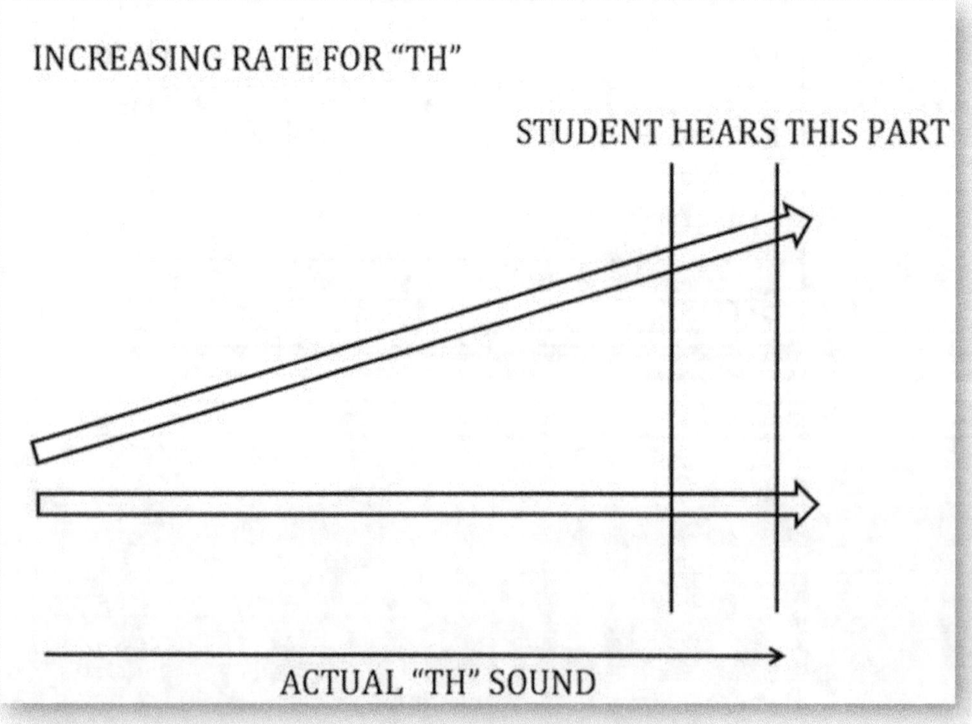

TH ASSOCIATION

Make a bursting action with your hand by opening it quickly from a closed position to indicate the increasing rate or burst. The buzz phrase INCREASE THE RATE can be used to remind the student to create the sound properly.

This sound must also be practiced with the **VOICE ON VOICE OFF** technique.

1. *Soon the drones cannot only see everything but think on their own too.*
2. *Both Seth and Anthony had doubts about withdrawing money from an unknown ATM*
3. *Bethany made them take out the needles smoothly so that it does not hurt.*
4. *The family therapy session they set up for Thursday was cancelled.*
5. *Although the weather wasn't nice, Meredith decided to go for a swim.*
6. *The three brothers each had different fathers and had nothing in common*
7. *We are both very thorough so we will thrive on this collaboration.*
8. *You can throw the balls to each other but don't pass it further than that column.*
9. *The thermometer at the hospital was filthy, therefore we threw it out.*
10. *I have been wondering for months whether or not he thinks of others or only himself.*

CONTIGUOUS WORDS (REMEMBER TO READ AS IF YOU ARE READING A SENTENCE)

TH Voice Off

Everything think Seth Anthony withdrawing Bethany therapy Thursday Meredith three nothing both thermometer filthy three months thinks

TH Voice On

The their them smoothly that they although the weather brothers fathers this the other further than that therefore whether others

TH ASSOCIATION QUIZ

So, what can you tell me about yourself?

Does this phrase sound familiar? Of course. It is the most frequently asked question in a new surrounding – if you are applying for a job or you have just started a new position but even when you meet your teacher for the first time, you can certainly expect this question.

Since people are going to form their opinion based on your answer, it is good to have an idea what you are going answer before the question is asked. Be prepared, write down what you are going to say, especially if you feel uncomfortable answering this question all the time, or you simply find it challenging to figure out what to say so that you give the right impression.

But how do you know what they want to hear? You don't. In fact, they probably don't have a clear idea what they would like to hear, either. They are simply interested in you and would like to get to know you better. Or, in the case of an interview or evaluation, for example, they pay attention not only to what you say but how you say it – what words, expressions you choose to use, how vague or detailed you are about different aspects of your life, whether or not you get into personal details or subjective matters. All this counts, and we have not even mentioned body language and tone of voice. A thorough interviewer forms his/her opinion by putting together these details. Most people, people who just would like to get to know you, do this subconsciously. They don't realize but they judge you based on all the above factors.

So, what can you tell me about yourself?

Does this phrase sound familiar? Of course. It is the most frequently asked questions in a new surrounding – if you are applying for a job or you have just started a new position but even when you meet your teacher for the first time, you can certainly expect this question.

Since people are going to form their opinion based on your answer, it is good to have an idea what you are going answer before the question is asked. Be prepared, write down what you are going to say, especially if you feel uncomfortable answering this question all the time, or you simply find it challenging to figure out what to say so that you give the right impression.

But how do you know what they want to hear? You don't. In fact, they probably don't have clear idea what they would like to hear, either. They are simply interested in you and would like to get to know you better. Or, in the case of an interview or evaluation, for example, they pay attention not only to what you say but how you say it – what words, expressions you choose to use, how vague or detailed you are about different aspects of your life, whether or not you get into personal details or subjective matters. All this counts, and we have not even mentioned body language and tone of voice. A thorough interviewer forms his/her opinion by putting together these details. Most people, people who just would like to get to know you, do this subconsciously. They don't realize but they judge you based on all the above factors.

Excerpt from *The Unicultural Advantage* by Andrew Miziniak (TH Slide 1-7)

TH SLIDE 1

When Transitory cultures think, they will either *understand or not understand* what they see. What they've seen has to either fit or not fit logically before they can process the data. They might not respond emotionally if an email reply comes back late. If someone said to you, don't go into that cave because it's dark, the darkness in your opinion is not a good enough reason not to investigate. In Transitory cultures, you will have to make your case. You will need to win their minds before you win their hearts.

But over time, all Transitory understandings become beliefs. What was once relegated to the spirited cortex of human intellect may eventually end up slumbering in the brain stem of an efficient human animal; one who prides him or herself on the efficiency of taking once wasteful understandings and cataloging them into knee-jerk and actionable beliefs. These are Complex cultures.

TH Voice On count: 16
Th Voice Off count: 1

TH SLIDE 2

When Complex cultures think, they will either *believe* or *not believe* what they see. It has to either fit or not fit emotionally before they can intellectually process the data. This means that in Complex cultures you will need to win their hearts before you can win their minds. You can't simply walk into a Complex culture, introduce yourself and get down to business because your title, job responsibility, or objective says to do so. You will need to win their trust. And that takes time.

Time not only creates relationships but also forms cultures and many of the rituals that go along with them. Over time, our understandings are slowly being cataloged and, perhaps in a genetic paradox of Mother Nature, blended into our fight or flight systems to allow us to react more quickly by not having to think. The paradox being that we go into a cultural slumber and stop thinking with our minds.

Can you imagine Sushi without wasabi? What started out as an Understanding – to find the tastiest way to rid the fish of bacteria and parasites - lathering it in Wasabi and soy sauce -has slowly turned into tradition that really has little purely logical need in today's world. There are many other tasty toppings you could put on fish but the habit remained. The notion of cultural slumber can be applied to something as benign as wasabi or Sushi to issues as complicated as how a culture treats women.

TH Voice On count: 24
TH Voice Off count: 7

TH SLIDE 3

Even if a culture is Transitory, the individuals you encounter may come from a Complex part of that Transitory culture. The exact inverse is also common; a Transitory individual in a Complex culture. This is why I feel that broadly labeling cultures as an absolute is dangerous. A person from Little Havana may be Complex but function in Transitory way because he or she lives and interacts in the US. The same is true for a Complex person from China going to a marketplace in Shanghai and interacting in a Transitory way.

TH Voice On Count: 6
TH Voice Off count: 0

TH SLIDE 4

These forces in our cultures can come from anywhere. The forces can be religious, spiritual, linguistic, regional, or political. Think about how Japan's culture was influenced by being isolated islands. Think about how Australia gained an advantage by possessing English as its language while being situated so far from the Western world. Think about how religions or mountains have carved cultural boundaries where people on one side are like us, and people on the other are barbarians.

TH Voice On Count: 5
TH Voice Off count: 3

TH SLIDE 5

History is littered with examples. We can see this by the effect the Hanseatic League of trading cities had on Europe in the Middle Ages, freeing up trade in otherwise disputed regions. We can see the effect of the Industrial Age driving brain drains from one culture into another. We can see the printing press forge paths to new religions and revolutions. These are resources either undermining previously strong forces or establishing new patterns of behaviors, as in the case of the Internet today.

TH Voice On Count: 10
TH Voice Off count: 1

TH SLIDE 6

Compare the American legal system to a Complex country where beliefs are firmly held by collectives. You will be amazed at how some countries pride themselves on capturing, arresting, convicting, and executing a criminal within a week while touting the efficiency of their legal system. Efficiency doesn't equal justice.

Tolerance will eventually become acceptance over time. This is the message of the brain stem telling us to get back to sleep, and for the sake of simplicity, to accept or not accept certain things. It just makes life so much easier.

TH Voice On Count: 6
TH Voice Off count: 2

TH SLIDE 7

Complex cultures are not wrong, they are simply being efficient. But when your efficiency impacts the lives of other free people, especially in an emerging global world, it is time to wake up.

To recap, Transitory cultures will tolerate or not tolerate your behavior and Complex cultures will either accept or not accept your behavior. Keep in mind that behavior is a representation of your attitude towards established values, which means that, depending on whether people are Transitory or Complex, they will either tolerate or accept your values.

TH Voice On Count: 9
TH Voice Off count: 0

ORCA TRIGGERS	
EE	△
Y	▽
UH	
TH	
Voice On/ Voice Off	
AW	
AH	!
O	
ER	[O]
Liaisons	⇨
Stress	

AW

IDENTIFICATION

Help the student understand that, unless there is a vowel coming afterward, there is no "L" sound in the AW sound. I like to remember the sound you make when you see a cute baby or a kitten; "awww."

Words with the AW sound include: austerity, always, awesome, fall.

AW ASSOCIATION

We use the buzz phrase DROP THE JAW or show a downward sliding pattern on our mouth. We can also remind them not to make an L sound. Please reference the symbol guide for the AW sound.

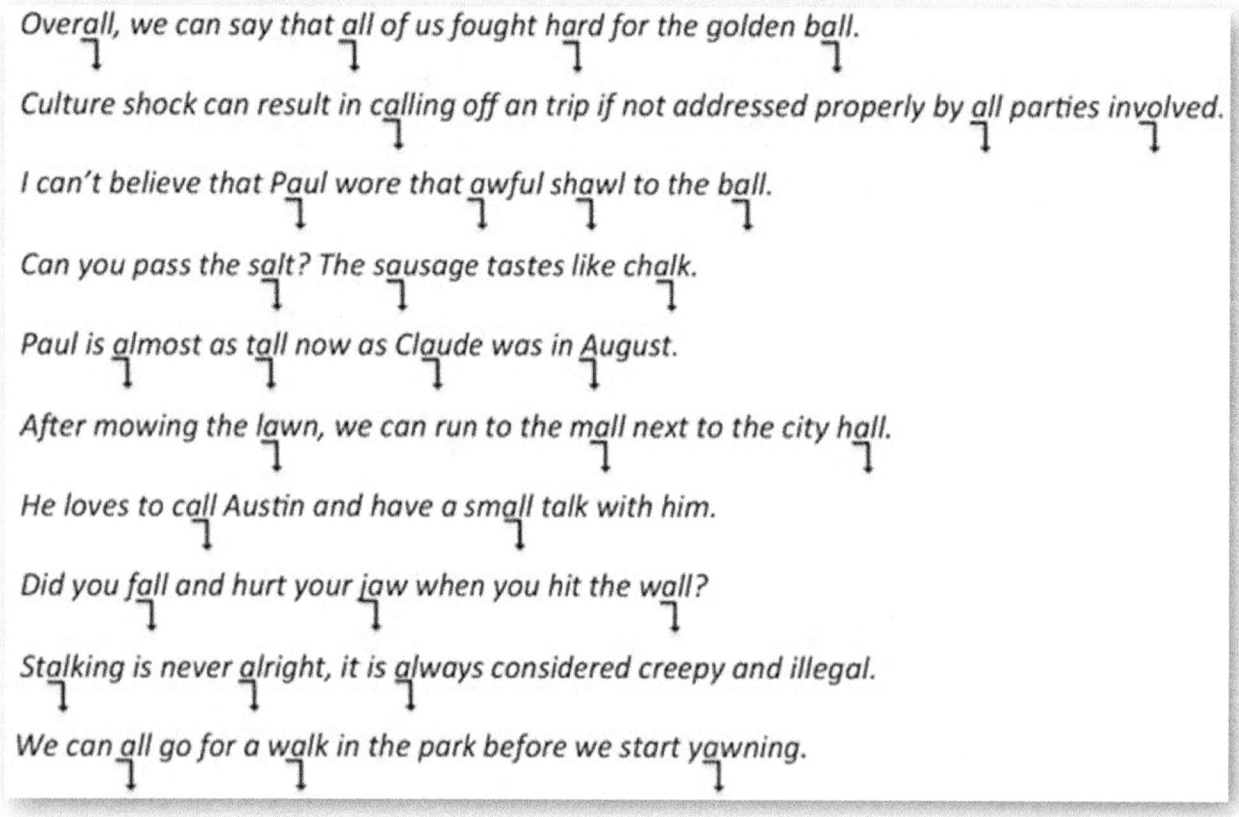

Overall, we can say that all of us fought hard for the golden ball.

Culture shock can result in calling off an trip if not addressed properly by all parties involved.

I can't believe that Paul wore that awful shawl to the ball.

Can you pass the salt? The sausage tastes like chalk.

Paul is almost as tall now as Claude was in August.

After mowing the lawn, we can run to the mall next to the city hall.

He loves to call Austin and have a small talk with him.

Did you fall and hurt your jaw when you hit the wall?

Stalking is never alright, it is always considered creepy and illegal.

We can all go for a walk in the park before we start yawning.

CONTIGUOUS WORDS (REMEMBER TO READ AS IF YOU ARE READING A SENTENCE)

Overall all hard ball calling all involved Paul awful shawl ball salt sausage chalk almost tall Claude August lawn mall hall call small fall law wall stalking alright always all walk yawning

AW ASSOCIATION QUIZ

So, what can you tell me about yourself?

Does this phrase sound familiar? Of course. It is the most frequently asked question in a new surrounding – if you are applying for a job or you have just started a new position but even when you meet your teacher for the first time, you can certainly expect this question.

Since people are going to form their opinion based on your answer, it is good to have an idea what you are going answer before the question is asked. Be prepared, write down what you are going to say, especially if you feel uncomfortable answering this question all the time, or you simply find it challenging to figure out what to say so that you give the right impression.

But how do you know what they want to hear? You don't. In fact, they probably don't have a clear idea what they would like to hear, either. They are simply interested in you and would like to get to know you better. Or, in the case of an interview or evaluation, for example, they pay attention not only to what you say but how you say it – what words, expressions you choose to use, how vague or detailed you are about different aspects of your life, whether or not you get into personal details or subjective matters. All this counts, and we have not even mentioned body language and tone of voice. A thorough interviewer forms his/her opinion by putting together these details. Most people, people who just would like to get to know you, do this subconsciously. They don't realize but they judge you based on all the above factors.

So, what can you tell me about yourself?

Does this phrase sound familiar? Of course. It is the most frequently asked questions in a new surrounding – if you are applying for a job or you have just started a new position but even when you meet your teacher for the first time, you can certainly expect this question.

Since people are going to form their opinion based on your answer, it is good to have an idea what you are going answer before the question is asked. Be prepared, write down what you are going to say, especially if you feel uncomfortable answering this question all the time, or you simply find it challenging to figure out what to say so that you give the right impression.

But how do you know what they want to hear? You don't. In fact, they probably don't have clear idea what they would like to hear, either. They are simply interested in you and would like to get to know you better. Or, in the case of an interview or evaluation, for example, they pay attention not only to what you say but how you say it – what words, expressions you choose to use, how vague or detailed you are about different aspects of your life, whether or not you get into personal details or subjective matters. All this counts, and we have not even mentioned body language and tone of voice. A thorough interviewer forms his/her opinion by putting together these details. Most people, people who just would like to get to know you, do this subconsciously. They don't realize but they judge you based on all the above factors.

Excerpt from *The Unicultural Advantage* by Andrew Miziniak (AW Slide 1-5)

AW SLIDE 1

Complex cultures use Time as a key mechanism in their lives. They engineer reality and use Belief as the basis for thinking. Things will be either believed or not believed. Have you ever tried to capture someone in a magical moment when all they see is an understanding of the situation? It's like entering into a religious ceremony with someone of a different faith when you've never experienced it before. Imagine someone who is not familiar with Christianity attending midnight mass and, while everyone is singing Christmas carols, they are wondering why there is a man nailed to a cross without proper clothing or why they use organs instead of a stereo. These seem like reckless and possibly offensive questions to someone who is part of the Complex environment, but if you are Transitory you are just trying to understand. If you are, however, from a different faith and locked into a Complex culture, you may not even accept what you see and feel an uneasiness about the entire experience of being in someone else's place of worship.

AW Count: 3

AW SLIDE 2

A Complex operating environment is built between individuals or groups that spend time together, share experiences, or homogenize in a particular way, such as sharing common values. The formation of a common bond in a Complex culture can be quickly accelerated by a common threat, as seen in cases of natural disasters, global crises, and acts of terrorism. Just by spending time, sharing experiences and sharing values together, we synthesize our perception of reality and can communicate more "efficiently." I use the word "efficiently" cautiously because, as previously discussed, a cultural slumber, where thoughts are relegated to the brain stem and reactions tend to be emotional, may seem efficient within the framework of low resources, but is not as adaptable to what we encounter in the diverse global world.

AW Count: 3

AW SLIDE 3

When Complex individuals spend a lot of time together they begin to synchronize to each other. This is what happens in relationships where you can immediately "read" the other person or know what an action means even if nothing is said directly. Small groups, as well as entire cultures, rely on this particular operating environment to maximize their rewards, success, and access to resources. Given enough time and limited resources, small groups of Complex cultures will gradually coalesce into massive, traditionally Complex cultures such as China, Saudi Arabia, or Japan.

The most personal example of a Complex environment is that of a family. Think back to the airport. When you are traveling and trying to get home, you don't necessarily have to be physically home to have the same interaction with your family. The dynamics of relationships between parents and children, husband and wife, brother and sister, remain in place and impose themselves no matter the surroundings.

AW Count: 5

AW SLIDE 4

I've seen the threshold for reactions to be much higher for Transitory cultures than for Complex. In a Transitory environment, you pretty much have to push the limits as far as you can by doing something that is absolutely not tolerated before you get a reaction. In a Complex environment, you only need to demonstrate a difference in accepted values to trigger a reaction.

This is an interesting paradox because it means you will be more warmly greeted in the South, in China, or in Saudi Arabia as long as your behavior doesn't trigger a threat to the accepted values. The reaction to a contradictory value trigger will be much more swift and aggressive.

The level of tolerance in a Transitory environment that does not hinge on a need to accept may seem cold at first glance. But the high level of tolerance actually provides a buffer for quite a large amount of diversity in the environment. That diversity is allowed to grow until certain tolerance levels are established. Those tolerance levels are enforced through laws and rules. The phrase "What you do in your bedroom is your business" is a typical representation of a Transitory mindset. In highly Complex cultures, they will attempt to be heavily involved in your private life.

AW Count: 6

AW SLIDE 5

To get a culture to fragment from Complex to Transitory you need only to add change, diversity, unpredictability, or a new resource. Simultaneously acceptance will fragment into tolerance, collectives into individuals, and beliefs will become understandings. Resources will be spent maintaining a cortex approach to society. Complex cultures want stability while Transitory cultures want change. Change is driven by energy, resources, and intensity, while stability is naturally driven by time. While cultures are made up of many components, they have very distinct driving forces. Transitory cultures are more driven by Energy; Complex cultures are more driven by Time.

Keep in mind, the way the terms Transitory and Complex are used to describe cultures and human interaction are specific to Unicultural. Do not get confused by whatever images, descriptions, or feelings those words may evoke from use in your everyday life.

To know thyself is to know if you are more Complex or more Transitory. Your Unicultural Advantage is to know if your environment rewards you more for being more tolerant or accepting than your really are. Before you can see the world around you, you will need to see yourself in this light. Then consider how it is we see, how we think, how we feel and what we do, and how the other culture does exactly the same thing and the cycle begins again. We are universally connected.

AW Count: 9

ORCA TRIGGERS	
EE	△
Y	▽
UH	
TH	
Voice On/ Voice Off	
AW	
AH	!
O	
ER	[O]
Liaisons	⇨
Stress	

AH

IDENTIFICATION

The AH pattern comes from the first part of the expression "Aaaa-Ha." Words like STOP, POP, and DROP carry with AH pattern. Please refer to OrcaMethod.com for identification help.

AH ASSOCIATION

We like to remind the student of the "a-ha" sound by using the "Surprise me!" buzzword or the symbol for the exclamation mark.

AH ASSOCIATION QUIZ

So, what can you tell me about yourself?

Does this phrase sound familiar? Of course. It is the most frequently asked question in a new surrounding – if you are applying for a job or you have just started a new position but even when you meet your teacher for the first time, you can certainly expect this question.

Since people are going to form their opinion based on your answer, it is good to have an idea what you are going answer before the question is asked. Be prepared, write down what you are going to say, especially if you feel uncomfortable answering this question all the time, or you simply find it challenging to figure out what to say so that you give the right impression.

But how do you know what they want to hear? You don't. In fact, they probably don't have a clear idea what they would like to hear, either. They are simply interested in you and would like to get to know you better. Or, in the case of an interview or evaluation, for example, they pay attention not only to what you say but how you say it – what words, expressions you choose to use, how vague or detailed you are about different aspects of your life, whether or not you get into personal details or subjective matters. All this counts, and we have not even mentioned body language and tone of voice. A thorough interviewer forms his/her opinion by putting together these details. Most people, people who just would like to get to know you, do this subconsciously. They don't realize but they judge you based on all the above factors.

So, what can you tell me about yourself?

Does this phrase sound familiar? Of course. It is the most frequently asked questions in a new surrounding – if you are applying for a job or you have just started a new position but even when you meet your teacher for the first time, you can certainly expect this question.

Since people are going to form their opinion based on your answer, it is good to have an idea what you are going answer before the question is asked. Be prepared, write down what you are going to say, especially if you feel uncomfortable answering this question all the time, or you simply find it challenging to figure out what to say so that you give the right impression.

But how do you know what they want to hear? You don't. In fact, they probably don't have clear idea what they would like to hear, either. They are simply interested in you and would like to get to know you better. Or, in the case of an interview or evaluation, for example, they pay attention not only to what you say but how you say it – what words, expressions you choose to use, how vague or detailed you are about different aspects of your life, whether or not you get into personal details or subjective matters. All this counts, and we have not even mentioned body language and tone of voice. A thorough interviewer forms his/her opinion by putting together these details. Most people, people who just would like to get to know you, do this subconsciously. They don't realize but they judge you based on all the above factors.

CONTIGUOUS WORDS (REMEMBER TO READ AS IF YOU ARE READING A SENTENCE)

About sound surrounding job down out how probably not how not body

AH Prep Test

Excerpt from *The Unicultural Advantage* by Andrew Miziniak (AH Slide 1-3)

AH SLIDE 1

Complex cultures use Time as a key mechanism in their lives. They engineer reality and use Belief as the basis for thinking. Things will be either believed or not believed. Have you ever tried to capture someone in a magical moment when all they see is an understanding of the situation? It's like entering into a religious ceremony with someone of a different faith when you've never experienced it before. Imagine someone who is not familiar with Christianity attending midnight mass and, while everyone is singing Christmas carols, they are wondering why there is a man nailed to a cross without proper clothing or why they use organs instead of a stereo. These seem like reckless and possibly offensive questions to someone who is part of the Complex environment, but if you are Transitory you are just trying to understand. If you are, however, from a different faith and locked into a Complex culture, you may not even accept what you see and feel an uneasiness about the entire experience of being in someone else's place of worship.

AH Count: 12

AH SLIDE 2

A Complex operating environment is built between individuals or groups that spend time together, share experiences, or homogenize in a particular way, such as sharing common values. The formation of a common bond in a Complex culture can be quickly accelerated by a common threat, as seen in cases of natural disasters, global crises, and acts of terrorism. Just by spending time, sharing experiences and sharing values together, we synthesize our perception of reality and can communicate more "efficiently." I use the word "efficiently" cautiously because, as previously discussed, a cultural slumber, where thoughts are relegated to the brain stem and reactions tend to be emotional, may seem efficient within the framework of low resources, but is not as adaptable to what we encounter in the diverse global world.

AH Count: 12

AH SLIDE 3

When Complex individuals spend a lot of time together they begin to synchronize to each other. This is what happens in relationships where you can immediately "read" the other person or know what an action means even if nothing is said directly. Small groups, as well as entire cultures, rely on this particular operating environment to maximize their rewards, success, and access to resources. Given enough time and limited resources, small groups of Complex cultures will gradually coalesce into massive, traditionally Complex cultures such as China, Saudi Arabia, or Japan.

The most personal example of a Complex environment is that of a family. Think back to the airport. When you are traveling and trying to get home, you don't necessarily have to be physically home to have the same interaction with your family. The dynamics of relationships between parents and children, husband and wife, brother and sister, remain in place and impose themselves no matter the surroundings.

AH Count: 12

ORCA TRIGGERS	
EE	△
Y	▽
UH	
TH	
Voice On/ Voice Off	
AW	
AH	!
O	
ER	[O]
Liaisons	⇨
Stress	

ISSUE

Again, we have the same issue with the O sound as we do with the Y and EE. Phonetic instructors will insist that there are many variations for you to learn as in:

- **/o_e/:**
  bode, bone, broke, broken, choke, chose, chrome, clone, close, clothes, clove, coke, cone, cope, cove, crone, dole, dome, dope, dose, dote, dose, dove, drone, drove, froze, frozen, globe, grope, hole, home, hone, hope, hose, hove, joke, lobe, lone, mode, mole
- **/oa/:**
  boat, coal, coat, coast, cocoa, download, foam, float, goat, groan, load, oak, moan, Oakland, oat, oatmeal, roach, road, roast, soak, soap, toad, toast
- **/ow/:**
  crow, elbow, follow, glow, grow, know, low, mow, own, owner, pillow, shadow, shallow, show, slow, snow, tow, window, yellow
- **/oe/:**
  doe, goes, hoe, oboe, toe, woe

The reality is that a non-native English speaker only needs one simple long O sound, and not all of these variations. We found in our research that the distance between the flat O and the long O is so great that it overpowers the need to study the variation between these phonetic pronunciations.

O IDENTIFICATION

If your O sound sounds flat, there is a simple adjustment and Orca tip to help you. To identify the proper round American O sound, you only need to take your own flat letter O and add a U sound to it.

O + U = OU and then say home, phone, alone, prone with that OU sound in the middle.

The variations that do need to be considered, however, exist in words spelled with the letter O but not pronounced with the long or short O.

Take this sentence for example:

"It doesn't make sense if it is our only obligation to offset the higher costs of commodities like coffee and milk at home."

The only two places we can apply the OU trigger in this sentence is with the words *only* and *home*. The other triggers include:

AH - The AH sound exists in words like our, obligation, logic, Ontario, contract, and constant – all spelled with the letter O. And also in words where it exists but is not spelled with O such as in *father*. Remember the trigger as well as the buzzword "Surprise me."

AW – You may recall the AW sound which also appears in words spelled with the letter O such as in "onward."

U – room, broom, to, do are also spelled with the letter O but the O sounds like a U.

O – This trigger is added now as it represents the O sound as in the words story, for, and chose, but should be carefully studied in the ER section for proper use in conjunction with the letter R.

UH – color, mother, and continued are spelled with the letter O but sound like the UH trigger.

Here's the same sentence exposing all the triggers in parentheses.

"It doesn't [UH] make sense if it is our only [OU] obligation [AH] to offset [AW] the higher costs [AW] of commodities [UH] like coffee [AW] and milk at home [OU]."

Here are a few more sentences to practice.

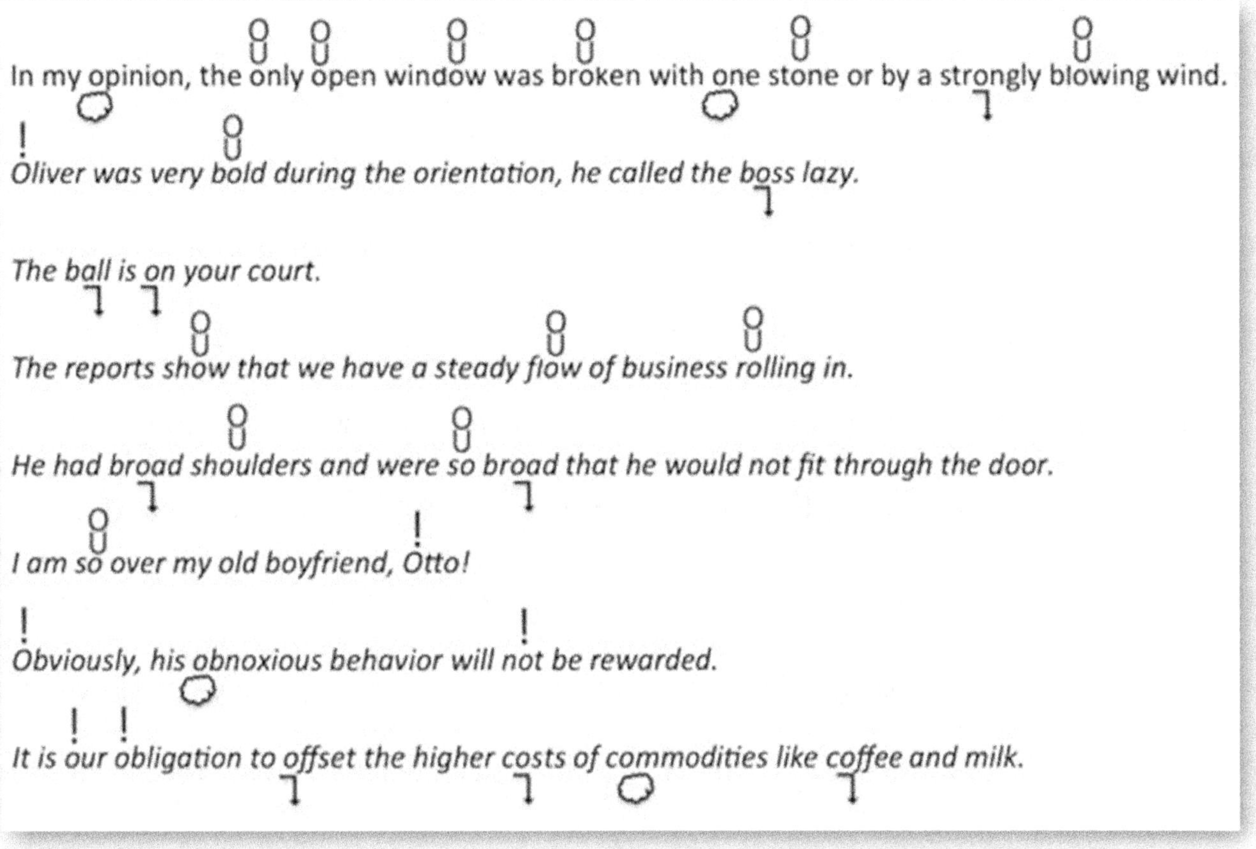

In my opinion, the only open window was broken with one stone or by a strongly blowing wind.

Oliver was very bold during the orientation, he called the boss lazy.

The ball is on your court.

The reports show that we have a steady flow of business rolling in.

He had broad shoulders and were so broad that he would not fit through the door.

I am so over my old boyfriend, Otto!

Obviously, his obnoxious behavior will not be rewarded.

It is our obligation to offset the higher costs of commodities like coffee and milk.

O ASSOCIATION

Associate the OU with the trigger "make it rounder" and wave your hand in a circle or use the symbol provided below. From this point on, the teacher will not say the sound anymore, but will instead remind you to take the two sounds and add them together to make the sound rounder.

Orchestration trigger is done by waving the hand in a circle and reminding the student where the O sound exists in spoken English. The teacher can also say "Make it rounder."

O ASSOCIATION QUIZ

Please use the OU, Uh, Ah, and Aw triggers for this one.

So, what can you tell me about yourself?

Does this phrase sound familiar? Of course. It is the most frequently asked question in a new surrounding – if you are applying for a job or you have just started a new position but even when you meet your teacher for the first time, you can certainly expect this question.

Since people are going to form their opinion based on your answer, it is good to a have an idea what you are going answer before the question is asked. Be prepared, write down what you are going to say, especially if you feel uncomfortable answering this question all the time, or you simply find it challenging to figure out what to say so that you give the right impression.

But how do you know what they want to hear? You don't. In fact, they probably don't a have clear idea what they would like to hear, either. They are simply interested in you and would like to get to know you better. Or, in the case of an interview or evaluation, for example, they pay attention not only to what you say but how you say it – what words, expressions you choose to use, how vague or detailed you are about different aspects of your life, whether or not you get into personal details or subjective matters. All this counts, and we have not even mentioned body language and tone of voice. A thorough interviewer forms his/her opinion by putting together these details. Most people, people who just would like to get to know you, do this subconsciously. They don't realize but they judge you based on all the above factors.

So, what can you tell me about yourself?

Does this phrase sound familiar? Of course. It is the most frequently asked questions in a new surrounding – if you are applying for a job or you have just started a new position but even when you meet your teacher for the first time, you can certainly expect this question.

Since people are going to form their opinion based on your answer, it is good to have an idea what you are going answer before the question is asked. Be prepared, write down what you are going to say, especially if you feel uncomfortable answering this question all the time, or you simply find it challenging to figure out what to say so that you give the right impression.

But how do you know what they want to hear? You don't. In fact, they probably don't have clear idea what they would like to hear, either. They are simply interested in you and would like to get to know you better. Or, in the case of an interview or evaluation, for example, they pay attention not only to what you say but how you say it – what words, expressions you choose to use, how vague or detailed you are about different aspects of your life, whether or not you get into personal details or subjective matters. All this counts, and we have not even mentioned body language and tone of voice. A thorough interviewer forms his/her opinion by putting together these details. Most people, people who just would like to get to know you, do this subconsciously. They don't realize but they judge you based on all the above factors.

O Prep Test

Please use O, Ou, Uh, Aw, Ah, and U triggers for this prep test.

Excerpt from *The Unicultural Advantage* by Andrew Miziniak (O Slide 1-5)

O SLIDE 1

True story. A director for a Fortune 500 company walked into a room to do a presentation for a dozen colleagues. This director was from Mexico and had just relocated to the United States. He prepared to highlight motivational management techniques by pointing to the strengths of the left and right brains in a team, identifying the logic of the left brain in contrast to the creative and artistic nature of the right brain.

He chose to use numbers and equations to represent the logical left brain and then drew a rainbow to represent the colorful and creative right brain. All of a sudden, a member of the audience, another manager, exclaimed, "I'm surprised you haven't been fired yet" and continued to react angrily at the representation used by the manager.

O Count: 4
U Count: 12
OU Count: 4
UH Count: 15
Aw Count: 2
AH Count: 4

O SLIDE 2

The Mexican manager was stunned. For the life of him, he didn't understand the problem. To him, a rainbow merely represented something benign and creative. Little did he know that this archetype had taken on significance in the U.S. as the symbol of the gay rights movement. Depending on the context, a rainbow is no longer just a rainbow. Luckily, the manager did not lose his job; some levelheaded colleagues calmed the situation and wrote it off as a cultural misunderstanding. And it was exactly that: a cultural misunderstanding. What lies behind it, however, is the reaction of each individual when they first saw the rainbow.

O Count: 1
U Count: 3
OU Count: 5
UH Count: 23
Aw Count: 6
AH Count: 5

O SLIDE 3

Cultural training has traditionally focused on behavior because that was all that could be seen. Trying to understand a culture through its behaviors is basically reverse engineering. But it may not be the best approach. It's like trying to learn a new language in a different way from the way you learned to speak your native tongue. You are insisting that it must be done in a different way. You see, as we all have our own culture, we already possess the tools to understanding the underlying forces of other cultures. Maybe not the behaviors, maybe not the rituals, but the forces and values.

O Count: 1
U Count: 12

OU Count: 4
UH Count: 15
Aw Count: 2
AH Count: 4

O SLIDE 4

Companies spend a lot of energy and capital trying to reverse engineer the behaviors of even a single culture to get an understanding of the meanings behind behaviors. The process of going from behaviors, to the emotions behind the behaviors, to finally understanding the meaning of the emotion behind the behavior is, to say the least, a daunting task.

In the case of a truly global corporation, to reverse engineer behaviors, each employee would need to have trainings tailored to them as well as to each person, group, culture, or region they may encounter.

But there are over 150 countries with thousands of regional variations and countless environments in which people interact. It becomes logistically, financially, and physically impossible to use this type of approach to prepare a corporation to function successfully at home and abroad with all of this variability. If you are just about to say you don't do business in 150 countries, then you probably never will.

O Count: 2
U Count: 18
OU Count: 2
UH Count: 31
Aw Count: 5
AH Count: 7

O SLIDE 5

Remember, diversity doesn't only exist outside your home culture. We tend to forget that in the U.S., by structuring work around rules and goals, companies aren't constantly reminded of the enormous tide of cultural diversity swelling under the surface. Some rules and goals can eliminate much of the visible diversity, but the cultural elements are still there.

In preparing the workforce for global interaction, the cultural training industry usually applies the reverse engineering approach, often leaving participants with a "deer in the headlights" reaction, not after the training, but when they have to put the training to use. A person will seem to know everything about a culture, yet has no idea of how, when, and where to act in unpredictable conditions.

O Count: 2
U Count: 8
OU Count: 3
UH Count: 25
Aw Count: 7
AH Count: 5

ORCA TRIGGERS	
EE	△
Y	▽
UH	
TH	
Voice On/ Voice Off	
AW	
AH	!
O	O U
ER	[O]
Liaisons	⇨
Stress	

Step 3

PUNCH IN PUNCH OUT the entire alphabet

A - ER	Air	pear	mare	stare
B - ER	Bermuda	bertha	amber	birthday
C – ER	Curd	anchor	curse	rancor
D – ER	Derma	anderson	flanders	understand
EE – ER	Ear	dear	near	clear
F – ER	Fur	loafer	furniture	stuffer
G – ER	Gershwin	anger	hunger	bugger
H – ER	Her	Hernia	Hurt	Herman
I – ER	Ire	Quagmire	Fire	Tire
J – ER	German	jerk	jersey	manger
K – ER	Kirby	Biker	Maker	Kernel
L – ER	Lurch	Learn	Butler	Mailer
M – ER	Mercantile	Summer	Mercedes	Merchant
N – ER	Nerf	Manner	Sinner	Nurse
O – ER	Or	Orchestrate	Enormous	Abnormal
P – ER	Percent	Temperate	Simper	Camper
S – ER	Surplus	Answer	Usurp	Servant
T – ER	Counter	Turtle	Turf	Terse
U – ER	Urine	Europe	Eureka	Your
V – ER	Vermin	Covert	Fervor	Verb
W – ER	Word	Tower	Sewer	Steward
X – ER	Elixir	Mixer	Exert	Boxer
Y – ER	Foyer	Layer	Lawyer	Conveyor
Z - ER	Loser	Laser	Zurich	appetizer

It is important to keep in mind that phonetic instructors will try to create separate ER categories such as:

- **/ar/:**
  armor, are, bar, barn, car, char, czar, far, farm, garland, jar, mar, par, scar, spar, star, tar, yarn
- **/er/:**
  dinner, farmer, ladder, letter, paper, hair, air, care, dare, fair, stare, scare, pear, rare, tear, wear, chair, share, there
- **/ir/:**

bird, birthday, circle, circus, girl, skirt

- **/or/:**
  corn, fork, horn, horse, north, torn
  four, store, core, door, more, floor, pour, shore, roar, soar, tore, wore, your, chore
- **/ur/:**
  church, hurt, purse, purple, turkey, turtle

Ignore these altogether, as every one of these ER sounds can be produced using the ORCA *Punch In Punch Out* technique.

IDENTIFICATION

Find the independent ER sound using the PUNCH IN PUNCH OUT technique.

Please refer to the sound in our practice section at OrcaMethod.com for assistance with sound identification.

ER ASSOCIATION

Associate the ER with the Buzz phrase "PUNCH IN PUNCH OUT" and then apply which sound is the PUNCH IN sound to associate. For example, for the word "fur," the trigger will look like [F], as well as:

Your [W]
Phrase [F]
Familiar [Y]
Burger [B]
Thirty [TH]
Together <u>[TH]</u> (underline the voiced, Voice On sound in the trigger)

ER ASSOCIATION QUIZ

So, what can you tell me about yourself?

Does this phrase sound familiar? Of course. It is the most frequently asked question in a new surrounding – if you are applying for a job or you have just started a new position but even when you meet your teacher for the first time, you can certainly expect this question.

Since people are going to form their opinion based on your answer, it is good to have an idea what you are going answer before the question is asked. Be prepared, write down what you are going to say, especially if you feel uncomfortable answering this question all the time, or you simply find it challenging to figure out what to say so that you give the right impression.

But how do you know what they want to hear? You don't. In fact, they probably don't a have clear idea what they would like to hear, either. They are simply interested in you and would like to get to know you better. Or, in the case of an interview or evaluation, for example, they pay attention not only to what you say but how you say it – what words, expressions you choose to use, how vague or detailed you are about different aspects of your life, whether or not you get into personal details or subjective matters. All this counts, and we have not even mentioned body language and tone of voice. A thorough interviewer forms his/her opinion by putting together these details. Most people, people who just would like to get to know you, do this subconsciously. They don't realize but they judge you based on all the above factors.

[W]
So, what can you tell me about yourself?

[F] [Y] [O] [F]
Does this phrase sound familiar? Of course. It is the most frequently

[S] [AW]
asked questions in a new surrounding – if you are applying for a job or you

[AW] [W] [CH] [O]
have just started a new position but even when you meet your teacher for the

[F] [S]
first time, you can certainly expect this question.

[A] [S]
Since people are going to form their opinion based on your answer, it

[S] [O]
is good to have an idea what you are going answer before the question is

[P] [A] [ER] [AW]
asked. Be prepared, write down what you are going to say, especially if you feel

[F] [S]
uncomfortable answering this question all the time, or you simply find it

[Y] [ER] [P]
challenging to figure out what to say so that you give the right impression.

[EE]
But how do you know what they want to hear? You don't. In fact, they

[P] [EE] [EE] [TH] [AW]
probably don't have clear idea what they would like to hear, either. They are

[T] [D] [O]
simply interested in you and would like to get to know you better. Or, in the

[T]
case of an interview or evaluation, for example, they pay attention not only to

[W] [P]
what you say but how you say it – what words, expressions you choose to use,

[F] [TH] [O]
how vague or detailed you are about different aspects of your life, whether or

[P] [D]
not you get into personal details or subjective matters. All this counts, and we

[TH]
have not even mentioned body language and tone of voice. A thorough

[T] [TH]
interviewer forms his/her opinion by putting together these details. Most

people, people who just would like to get to know you, do this subconsciously.

[ER] [T]
They don't realize but they judge you based on all the above factors.

Excerpt from *The Unicultural Advantage* by Andrew Miziniak (ER Slide 1-8)

ER SLIDE 1

It's much easier to prepare for culture shock abroad in environments drastically different from our own because visible differences are much easier to identify. This is why some American companies assume you will need cultural training coming from the United States to China, but not necessarily to a country like Canada or Australia.

ER SLIDE 2

You typically know when you will be entering a new environment and therefore are able to prepare for the transition. But what about here at home? Some Americans don't think they need cultural training if they are working in the U.S. and not relocating because it's their own culture. But what happens when cultural change occurs around you, without your input or choice? What if your neighborhood, town, or city radically changes from an influx of multicultural people? And even more difficult, when that change is gradual, by the time you realize it's happened, it's already too late for you to adapt in a comfortable manner. In that case, even in your own culture, own town, own neighborhood, you can experience culture shock.

ER SLIDE 3

Look at it this way. Imagine 3 cars are going down a road at 55mph. The car on the left is doing 55mph because just last week the driver got a speeding ticket and doesn't want to go faster. The one in the middle is going 55mph because his car is broken and can't go any faster. And the one on the right is going 55mph because he believes in the rule of law, the speed limit.

If you're from a culture that likes to circumvent authority, you may go to each of the drivers and say, "Hey, I know there's no police ahead, you're fine to speed." The guy on the left who had the speeding ticket will thank you and speed off. The guy in the middle will only thank you and smile because he feels embarrassed that he can't really go any faster. And the guy on the right will be offended by your asking him to break the rule of law.

ER SLIDE 4

Sometimes an identical behavior can be driven by very differing values. This is why it is critical for cultural support to be mandatory and not elective. When it is elective, we are propagating the myth that cultures are about behaviors and not about values. We tend to rate cultures by their seeming difference from us on a behavioral level. Even cultural training companies do it by constantly highlighting the differences among us. The truth is that there may be just as many differences under the surface of a culture that is seemingly identical to ours.

ER SLIDE 5

In order to properly adapt to a global world we need to go beyond behaviors. With so much riding on getting business right the first time, this is not an inconsequential matter.

A key Unicultural advantage is knowing that all individuals may experience culture shock. It's not just the visible artifacts, stress, and discomfort that should be our indicators for concern. Just as we shouldn't judge an individual's adaptation by external factors, we need to learn to be cautious about judging another culture by its visible differences. This is a key component to successfully navigating relationships.

As for relocation, we also have the advantage of knowing not to take the relocating assignee by their word when it comes to adaptation. There has to be a "release" process implemented in order to give the green light. Training and awareness is the answer to this.

ER SLIDE 6

Consider that an assignee might tell you they are fine, but doesn't reveal that their spouse or kids are struggling with the relocation. This is a real matter for concern. What typically happens with High Frequency assignees with partners that are Low Frequency is that they try to paint the big picture to their spouse. They say "Come on, look at the opportunity, the kids are learning Chinese, they are paying for the move, we get a free ride to explore China, why are you complaining about not having a garden when I'm working all the time and I have enough stress to deal with?" The Low Frequency individual is being punished for having culture shock. Think of the burden on this person.

ER SLIDE 7

Not only is the actual culture shock a punishment, but then the spouse adds to it by expecting more stability at home. The Low Frequency spouse feels as if they have let down their partner by not being able to provide a feeling of stability and home to the relationship. It's a double whammy.

If we don't mandate support, we are creating undue stresses on employees and their families. It's not just people that are High and Low frequency. High Frequency companies can punish Low Frequency employees in international business scenarios, when the Low Frequency individuals can't adapt fast enough to change. The remedy is multi-national team training.

ER SLIDE 8

As for non-relocating multi-national teams here at home, similar adaptation strategies can be employed to get a proper integration and interactive workplace.

Take a look at yourself and try to figure out if you are low or high frequency. Would you be ok packing your bags tonight and starting work in Shanghai tomorrow? What would you take with you to be happy? What would you need to feel whole?

And what if you're never planning to relocate, but the cultural landscape of your town or neighborhood changes, will you be ready to meet these challenging scenarios? Identifying how you react to change is a big step forward for both the parties moving in and the host culture.

ORCA TRIGGERS	
EE	△
Y	▽
UH	
TH	
Voice On/ Voice Off	
AW	
AH	!
O	
ER	[O]
Liaisons	⇨
Stress	

ISSUE

Students try to pronounce both the T and the R together.

TR DR IDENTIFICATION

To the teacher: ask the student if they have a CH sound in their native language. They usually do such as *chiba* in Japanese, *chico* in Spanish, and *cicho* in Polish. If they do not, you will need to find the sound. Tell them the new rule is that all TR combinations are pronounced CH and all DR combinations are pronounced J as in Jerry.

To the student: from now on, most words that start with TR will begin with the "CH" sound and words that begin with DR will be pronounced with the "J" sound.

TD DR ASSOCIATION

The buzz phrase is TR DR RULE

The TR DR Rule is a subset of the ER pattern so it is not considered its own pattern in the system. We do, however, provide you with a trigger you can use to correct yourself which is CH and J over the word. Then, simply punch in and out the CH and J sounds where appropriate.

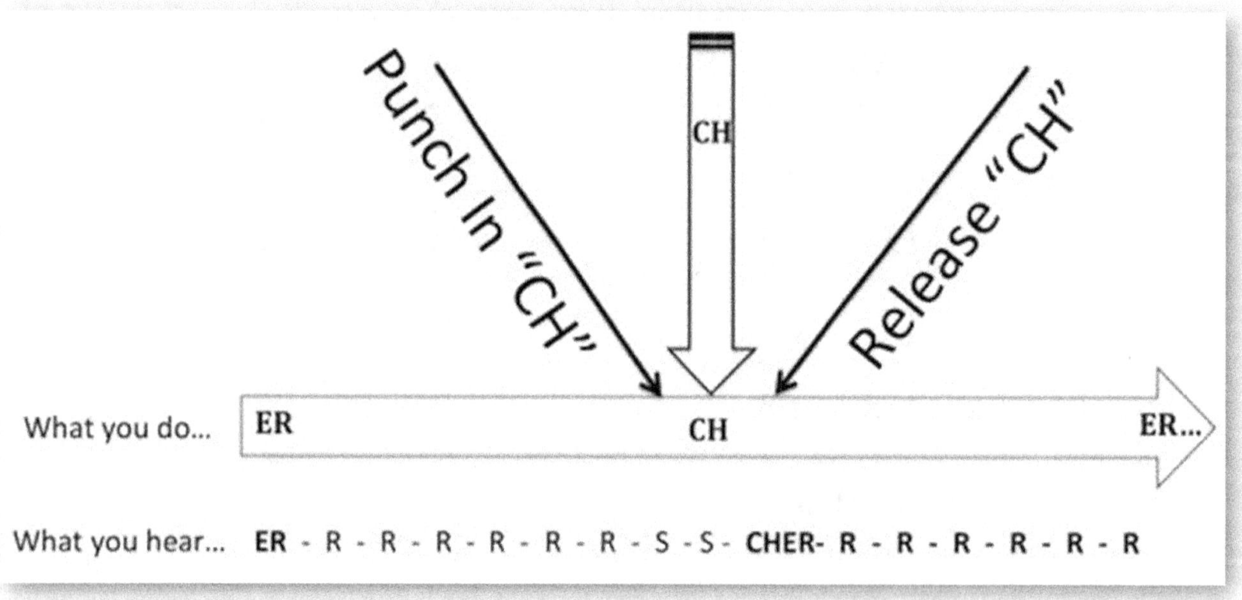

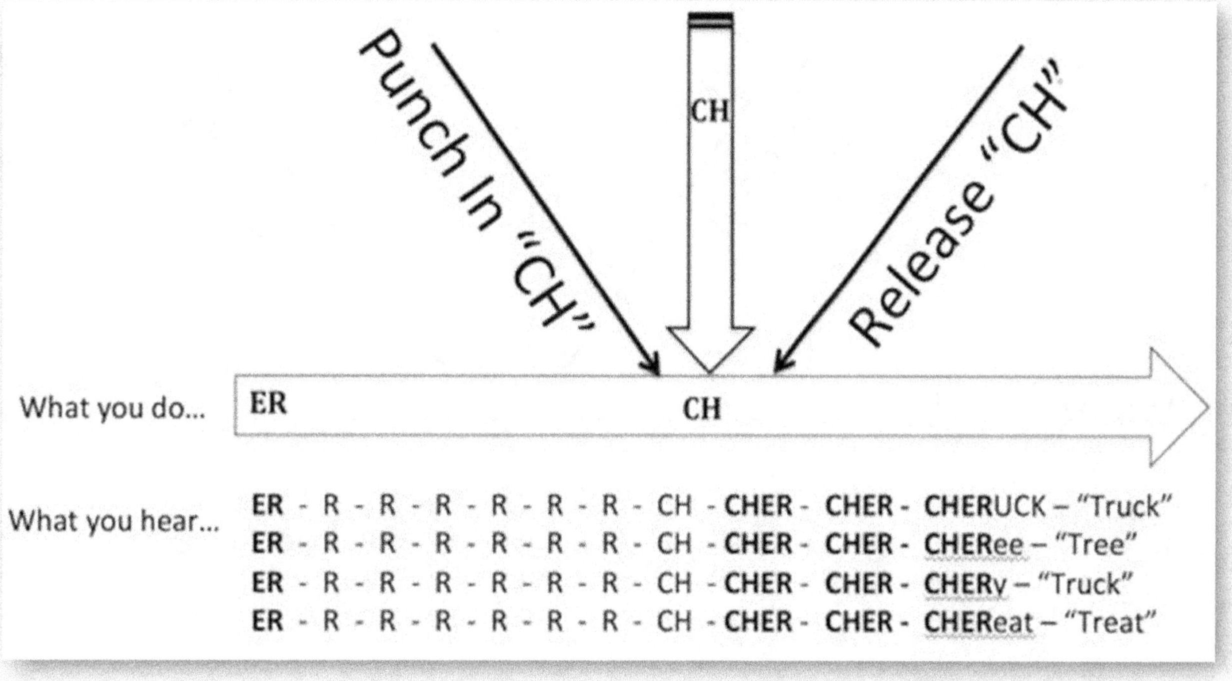
Punch In "CH"
CH
Release "CH"
What you do...
ER
CH
What you hear...
ER - R - R - R - R - R - R - CH - CHER - CHER - CHERUCK – "Truck"
ER - R - R - R - R - R - R - CH - CHER - CHER - CHERee – "Tree"
ER - R - R - R - R - R - R - CH - CHER - CHER - CHERy – "Truck"
ER - R - R - R - R - R - R - CH - CHER - CHER - CHEReat – "Treat"

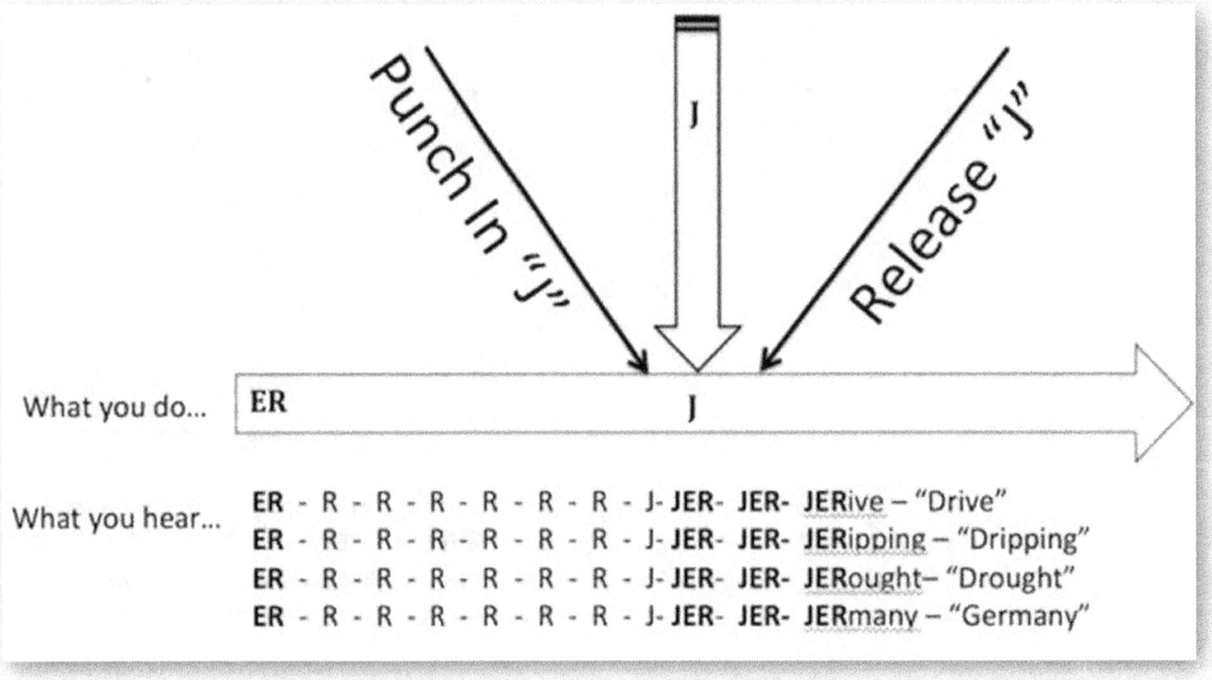
Punch In "J"
J
Release "J"
What you do...
ER
J
What you hear...
ER - R - R - R - R - R - R - J- JER- JER- JERive – "Drive"
ER - R - R - R - R - R - R - J- JER- JER- JERipping – "Dripping"
ER - R - R - R - R - R - R - J- JER- JER- JERought– "Drought"
ER - R - R - R - R - R - R - J- JER- JER- JERmany – "Germany"

TR DR Slide 1 (Located in the ER Practice Section on OrcaMethod.com)

Trevor trained a truck driver to dry dripping drains. He tried and tried but couldn't get the drenched drains to stop leaking. Treating it like a puzzle, he drew a diagram and managed to dry the floor by fixing the drip.

ORCA TRIGGERS	
EE	△
Y	▽
UH	
TH	
Voice On/ Voice Off	 
AW	
AH	!
O	
ER	[O]
Liaisons	⇨
Stress	

ISSUE

Native American-English speakers often do not pronounce each word succinctly and individually. They often rely on a smooth flowing pattern of sounds of words that are bound by Liaisons. In the phrase, "This is only" the actual sound the non-speaker hears is, "Dy Sizonelee" and the confusion makes them begin ultra-processing possible meanings while the conversation continues. This ultra processing is one of the reasons it is difficult to maintain high-speed conversations in English; the non-native speaker is always playing catch-up. "Your English" sounds like "Yoo Rynglish."

Liaisons Identification

Unless there is a comma or a natural pause, such as for a breath, a Liaison will occur in typical speech when the last consonant of a word begins the next word that begins with either a vowel, or a vowel sound.

Take the last consonant and start the next word with it. For example:

"This is" becomes "Thi Sis"
"Your English" becomes "You Renglish"
"Figure out" becomes "Figu Rout"

Be cautious, because some words may end in a vowel such as an E but still carry over the consonant before it if the vowel is silent. Examples of this are: "one is" becomes the sound "wuNyyz." Just carry the N and start the word IS with the N.

"Believe in" is another phrase where it ends with a vowel but, because the vowel is silent, we make a liaison to the V and start the word with that sound, making the final sound "beleeVin."

Another is "place is" which sounds like "playSiz."

LIAISONS ASSOCIATION

We use the buzz phrase "liaison" or "connect the two" by making a finger gesture – a half circle back and forth to indicate the connection between the two words. For symbol triggers, we use the arrow to indicate the carryover of the sound.

Read the same text while orchestrating the previous correction and add the hand gesture and buzzword to fix the flow of the liaisons. It may be necessary to slow down the speech to get it right.

*A word of caution about liaisons: we reserved the right of discretion where natural pauses should occur in a sentence, so there may be a couple instances where there is technically a consonant before the next vowel but it just didn't sound right to be connected.

LIAISONS ASSOCIATION QUIZ

So, what can you tell me about yourself?

Does this phrase sound familiar? Of course. It is the most frequently asked question in a new surrounding – if you are applying for a job or you have just started a new position but even when you meet your teacher for the first time, you can certainly expect this question.

Since people are going to form their opinion based on your answer, it is good to have an idea what you are going answer before the question is asked. Be prepared, write down what you are going to say, especially if you feel uncomfortable answering this question all the time, or you simply find it challenging to figure out what to say so that you give the right impression.

But how do you know what they want to hear? You don't. In fact, they probably don't have a clear idea what they would like to hear, either. They are simply interested in you and would like to get to know you better. Or, in the case of an interview or evaluation, for example, they pay attention not only to what you say but how you say it – what words, expressions you choose to use, how vague or detailed you are about different aspects of your life, whether or not you get into personal details or subjective matters. All this counts, and we have not even mentioned body language and tone of voice. A thorough interviewer forms his/her opinion by putting together these details. Most people, people who just would like to get to know you, do this subconsciously. They don't realize but they judge you based on all the above factors.

So, what can you tell me about yourself?

Does this phrase sound familiar? Of course. It is the most frequently asked questions in a new surrounding – if you are applying for a job or you have just started a new position but even when you meet your teacher for the first time, you can certainly expect this question.

Since people are going to form their opinion based on your answer, it is good to have an idea what you are going to answer before the question is asked. Be prepared, write down what you are going to say, especially if you feel uncomfortable answering this question all the time, or you simply find it challenging to figure out what to say so that you give the right impression.

But how do you know what they want to hear? You don't. In fact, they probably don't have clear idea what they would like to hear, either. They are simply interested in you and would like to get to know you better. Or, in the case of an interview or evaluation, for example, they pay attention not only to what you say but how you say it – what words, expressions you choose to use, how vague or detailed you are about different aspects of your life, whether or not you get into personal details or subjective matters. All this counts, and we have not even mentioned body language and tone of voice. A thorough interviewer forms his/her opinion by putting together these details. Most people, people who just would like to get to know you, do this subconsciously. They don't realize but they judge you based on all the above factors.

Excerpt from *The Unicultural Advantage* by Andrew Miziniak (Liaisons Slide 1-4)

LIAISONS SLIDE 1

Transitory and Complex cultures possess specific systems by which they process meanings, which create what we will now call *Operating Environments*. Think of Operating Environments as the operating system in your computer. Some, like Mac OS, are designed to be approachable by literally anyone, while systems like Linux favor the programmers that know how to install, navigate, and alter the environment. Mac OS is a predictable environment, which allows for unpredictable people to use it. Even a child can navigate the interface of an iPad. Linux is an unpredictable environment that prefers homogenized programmers or those who are more specialized to use it. Sure, the system can be used to create simple interfaces, but it is not designed to be completely predictable for those who do not understand how it works.

LIAISONS Count: 31

LIAISONS SLIDE 2

Every interaction we have with another person takes place within one of these two operating environments, whether Transitory or Complex. To what degree it is Transitory and Complex depends on the culture with which you interact. The Transitory Operating Environment is the environment used in situations where there has not yet been time spent together, no shared experiences, and no shared values. This is any type of environment where people come together to exchange. The Transitory OE is our operating environment for many social situations and is driven by change, diversity, and the unpredictability of people. Big cities, corporations, marketplaces, legal systems, and airports are all examples of these Transitory environments.

LIAISONS Count: 23

LIAISONS SLIDE 3

An airport serves as a Transitory environment by its very nature -- transferring people from one place to the next. Everyone is moving around interacting, but the environment dictates the interaction. Everyone must clearly identify themselves and make themselves predictable. Warnings are read aloud over speakers with rules repeated for those who may just not know.

Everyone is on his or her way to a destination and no one is there to loiter. Or any loitering that does take place is with the clear purpose of waiting for a flight. You can't even get into the terminal without a clearly marked boarding pass.

Transitory environments, just like airports, rely on rules, structures, and goals to accomplish their tasks and do not rely heavily on relationships with you. They do not need time spent with you; they need your energy to follow the system.

LIAISON Count: 22

LIAISONS SLIDE 4

Even if you manage to build a relationship in this Transitory state, it may still be perilous, fruitless, or misleading. We've all experienced those moments during a flight, train ride, or at an airport bar, when we engage with someone to great depths, trade stories, discuss issues and share experiences. Even with hours spent talking and contact information exchanged with promises to one day meet up, we never do see each other again. What happened there? Why did the relationship fizzle?

Or worse, what if that person contacts you when you are back in the rhythm of your everyday life? Will you feel pressured to invite them, basically a stranger, into the privacy of your own home?

Understanding how to manage Transitory OE's will shine light on human interaction and why certain relationships grow and others fizzle. Since American culture is structured in a Transitory fashion, it is important for us to understand how we are seen by individuals coming from Complex cultures.

LIAISON Count: 35

ORCA TRIGGERS	
EE	△
Y	▽
UH	
TH	
Voice On/ Voice Off	
AW	
AH	!
O	O U
ER	[O]
Liaisons	⇨
Stress	

ISSUE

ESL students often put the stress on the wrong part of the word such as at the end of the word in French, or syllabically as in Japanese. Their result is a word that sounds like engineer or En Gi Neer instead of ENgineer or prodUCT instead of PROduct.

STRESS IDENTIFICATION

The majority of stress in English comes from the beginning or middle of the word. For the purpose of simplicity and, in order to avoid putting a trigger on every single word, we will try to isolate the stress triggers to words that are more commonly mispronounced. You can do stress exercises with the triggers with one of our teachers if you would like more practice.

STRESS ASSOCIATION

Associate with the buzz phrase STRESS ON THE MIDDLE or STRESS ON THE BEGINNING

We've only chosen select longer words to assist you, but the general rule stands that most stress in American English is at the beginning or middle of the word. Pay close attention to exactly where the lightning bolt arrow points as that is the sound with more emphasis.

So, what can you tell me about yourself? (EE & Y

Does this phrase sound familiar? Of course. It is the most frequently asked questions in a new surrounding – if you are applying for a job or you have just started a new position but even when you meet your teacher for the first time, you can certainly expect this question.

Since people are going to form their opinion based on your answer, it is good to have idea what you are going answer before the question is asked. Be prepared, write down what you are going to say, especially if you feel uncomfortable answering this question all the time, or you simply find it challenging to figure out what to say so that you give the right impression.

But how do you know what they want to hear? You don't. In fact, they probably don't have clear idea what they would like to hear, either. They are simply interested in you and would like to get to know you better. Or, in the case of an interview or evaluation, for example, they pay attention not only to what you say but how you say it – what words, expressions you choose to use, how vague or detailed you are about different aspects of your life, whether or not you get into personal details or subjective matters. All this counts, and we have not even mentioned body language and tone of voice. A thorough interviewer forms his/her opinion by putting together these details. Most people, people who just would like to get to know you, do this subconsciously. They don't realize but they judge you based on all the above factors.

INSTRUCTOR VOCAL TRIGGER REVIEW SHEET

Use these vocal triggers in conjunction with our trigger symbols to assist your student in corrections.

Sound Pattern	Vocal Trigger
Y & EE	Go Lower, Go Higher
ER	Punch In Punch Out
O	Make it Rounder
TH	Increase the Rate
S&Z/ F&V	Voice On Voice Off
TR DR	TR DR Rule
Liaisons	Connect the ...
Stress	Stress at... Beginning. Middle, End
AAH	Drop the Jaw

Conclusion

Congratulations on working through this book. You may be one of the many who needed a shortcut through the endless maze of checklists that the English experts out there would have you do in order to improve your accent. It's like having to go on a tour of Paris every day to enjoy the city when all you want is just to make Paris a part of you. But these "tours" of the English language have no end and the experts waste our valuable time and money on something they tell us is real. I don't want to take away from the good people who try to help as classes are often fun and entertaining, but to properly improve your English, you must interact with the language in a different way than everyone else. The Orca Method™ gives you that advantage with our 9 steps to practice for better fluency.

You won't leave this book with complicated systems and theories but with a simple approach that will always work for you and be a part of you. I have designed this as a cure rather than just a treatment. I have made it simple because I believe it *is* simple. Keep practicing and you will see the changes occur and, if you need a bit of assistance, help is available right on the net. Just be sure it's the Orca Method that you apply.

Best wishes and good luck.

NOTES:

NOTES:

NOTES:

www.ingramcontent.com/pod-product-compliance
Lightning Source LLC
Chambersburg PA
CBHW081827230426
43668CB00017B/2400
* 9 7 8 0 6 9 2 6 0 7 6 4 0 *